EUROPE
LOOKS
AT THE
CIVIL WAR

EUROPE
LOOKS
AT THE
CIVIL WAR

An Anthology *Edited by*

Belle Becker Sideman and Lillian Friedman

The Orion Press

New York

For Abner and Toby

CONTENTS

xvi

PREFACE

This book begins with a death and ends with a death. John Brown was hanged and Abraham Lincoln was shot. In between these two deaths hundreds of thousands of young American men fought and froze and starved and died. And while all this was happening did the rest of the world think about it, care about it, do anything about it? The editors hope that some answers to these questions will be found in the following pages.

A century ago perceptive and visionary Europeans anticipated America's role as a world power. "There is no such thing as distance today," Count Agénor de Gasparin said in 1861, depending upon the point of view, "the young giant across the Atlantic" was going to become either a world threat or a trailblazer for enlightened democracy.

The editors knew they could not reveal in this book what England thought, what France thought, what Russia thought. Countries do not think. But the individual European—the Scotsman whose sympathy was with the North though a Confederate defeat would ruin him financially; the French poet who excoriated the North because a former mistress had to flee her Southern home; the Russian diplomat married to an American woman; the British correspondent, so dazzled by the sight of Negroes in splendid attire that he wrote, "Can these people really be slaves?"—and scores of other such intensely personal reactions are the lifeblood of this book. A wide variety of Europeans, aristocrats and revolutionists, churchmen and kings, poets and statesmen came vividly alive as they expressed their feelings about the greatest war of the century. Thus this anthology is a reflection of human reactions, sometimes calm, sometimes inflamed, often intertwined with the religious, social and political interests of the subject.

Many months of research and checking here and abroad produced evidence of the extent to which Europe was involved politically, materially and emotionally in our Civil War. To Europeans it was a crucial, sometimes day-by-day drama, commented upon and written about as the events unfolded. Long-forgotten and out-of-print diplomatic memoirs, collections of letters, Ph.D. theses, newspaper files in the New York Public Library, the Library of Congress, the British Museum and the Bibliothèque Nationale provided the material for this book, much of which, we hope, will uncover new facets of American history.

The reader will note a certain amount of dependence on official documents, newspaper reports, speeches and letters. Not many books were written about the war while it was still going on. But countless articles, letters and pamphlets were written and speeches made in the heat of the moment. It was to these sources that the editors went and nothing written or said after 1865 appears in this book.

Some explanation is due the reader for the glaring inconsistencies in spelling, capitalization and punctuation. Except for the material translated especially for this volume, the editors have followed the style and usage of all the original sources. One other exception has been made: the word Negro is capitalized throughout. Occasional departures from the chronological order of the text occur when the editors wished to maintain the continuity of ideas or comments by the person quoted. There has been absolutely no tampering with original texts except when deletions were made, and these are indicated by the usual three and four dots.

Since the editors are neither scholars nor historians, the determining factor in choosing the selections was always the human-interest appeal and a desire to communicate some of their own excitement and fascination with the subject. For that reason the omission of descriptions of battles is deliberate and not an oversight. These aspects of the war the editors happily leave to the experts who to this day are still disputing why and how a battle was won or lost. At best we are fully aware that a work of such formidable scope could only emerge as a fragmentary picture.

In this book will be found both friendly and unfriendly voices. Among the latter, the wish and belief most often expressed was that the United States could never again exist as one nation. Fortunately they were wrong. The Civil War was the last internecine war fought on our soil.

B.B.S.

L.F.

EUROPE
LOOKS
AT THE
CIVIL WAR

"I FALL ON MY KNEES, WEEPING"

As poet, novelist and playwright, Victor Hugo dominated the Romantic movement in France during the middle of the nineteenth century. As a liberal republican and representative in the National Assembly, Hugo played an important role in the affairs of his country until he went into voluntary exile (1851–1870) in protest against the coup d'état of Napoleon III. Staunch defender of liberty, he exerted a powerful moral influence on most of the political controversies of his time. Curiously enough, not much is known about Hugo's attitude during the Civil War itself. John Brown seems to have struck his imagination to a much greater degree than Lincoln, whom he certainly admired. He completed *Les Miserables* in 1862 and his conception of Jean Valjean probably owes a great deal to the august figure of John Brown. Hugo's own words would seem to suggest as much: "I myself prefer a man who becomes the martyr of his cause to one who succeeds. John Brown is greater than Washington, and Pisacane [Italian revolutionary who died while trying to liberate Ponza in 1852] is greater than Garibaldi. Somebody must stand up for the vanquished." The news of John Brown's trial and death sentence reached Hugo on December 1, 1859, and with it came the false report of a reprieve. Hugo's immediate reaction was his now-famous *"Appeal for John Brown."* Its publication was followed by an exchange of letters between Hugo and various friends as well as with political figures of the period.

"Appeal for John Brown"

Hauteville House, December 2, 1859

To the Editor of the London *News:*

. . . A white man, a free man . . . John Brown endeavored to commence the work of emancipation by the liberation of slaves in Virginia. Pious, austere, animated with the old Puritan spirit, inspired by the spirit of the Gospel, he sounded to these men, these oppressed brothers, the rallying cry of Freedom. The slaves, enervated by servitude, made no response to the appeal. Slavery afflicts the soul with weakness. Brown, though deserted, still fought at the head of a handful of heroic men; he was riddled with balls; his two young sons, sacred martyrs, fell dead at his side, and he himself was taken. This is what they call the affair at Harper's Ferry.

John Brown has been tried, with four of his comrades, Stephens, Coppic, Green and Copeland. . . .

Such things cannot be done with impunity in the face of the civilized world. The universal conscience of humanity is an ever-watchful eye. Let the judges of Charles Town, and Hunter and Parker, and the slaveholding jurors, and the whole population of Virginia, ponder it well: they are watched! They are not alone in the world. At this moment, America attracts the eyes of the whole of Europe.

John Brown, condemned to die, was to have been hanged on the 2nd of December—this very day. But news has just reached us. A respite has been granted to him. It is not until the 16th that he is to die.

A single State ought not to have the power to dishonor all the rest, and in this case there is an obvious

5

justification for a federal intervention. Otherwise, by hesitating to interfere when it might prevent a crime, the Union becomes a participator in its guilt. No matter how intense may be the indignation of the generous Northern States, the Southern States force them to share the opprobrium of this murder. All of us, no matter who we may be, who are bound together as compatriots by the common tie of a democratic creed, feel ourselves in some measure compromised. If the scaffold should be erected on the 16th of December, the incorruptible voice of history would thence forward testify that the august Confederation of the New World had added to all its rites of holy brotherhood a brotherhood of blood. . . .

When we reflect on what Brown, the liberator, the champion of Christ, has striven to effect, and when we remember that he is about to die, slaughtered by the American Republic, the crime assumes an importance co-extensive with that of the nation which commits it—and when we say to ourselves that this nation is one of the glories of the human race; that, like France, like England, like Germany, she is one of the great agents of civilization; that she sometimes even leaves Europe in the rear by the sublime audacity of some of her progressive movements; that she is the Queen of an entire world, and that her brow is irradiated with a glorious halo of freedom, we declare our conviction that John Brown will not die; for we recoil horror-struck from the idea of so great a crime committed by so great a people.

Viewed in a political light, the murder of Brown would be an irreparable fault. It would penetrate the Union with a gaping fissure which would lead in the end to its entire disruption . . . it is certain that it would shake to its centre the entire fabric of American democracy. You preserve your infamy, but you sacrifice your glory. . . .

As for myself, though I am but a mere atom, yet being, as I am, in common with all other men, inspired with the conscience of humanity, I fall on my knees, weeping before the great starry banner of the New World; and with clasped hands, and with profound and filial respect, I implore the illustrious American Republic, sister of the French Republic, to see to the safety of the universal moral law, to save John Brown, to demolish the threatening scaffold of the 16th of December, and not to suffer that beneath its eyes, and I add, with a shudder, almost by its fault, a crime should be perpetrated surpassing the first fratricide in iniquity.

For—yes, let America know it, and ponder on it well—there is something more terrible than Cain slaying Abel: It is Washington slaying Spartacus!

Victor Hugo, LETTERS ON AMERICAN SLAVERY

Excerpt from a letter to C. Caraguel, journalist and theatre critic of *Charivari.* This paper actively supported Lincoln and the cause of emancipation all through the war. Caraguel quoted Hugo's "Appeal" in an article dated December 11, 1859.

December 18, 1859

Just as I was reading your laudatory note on my appeal in favor of John Brown, I received a most horrible piece of news. The murder has been com-

7

mitted, the reprieve was a lie. John Brown was hung on December 2nd. . . . To think that such an infamous crime should have taken place in a republic! Now that the deed is done, let us await the consequences; events have a logic all their own, even though democracies may have none, as you say so well. The question is now clearly posed, slavery must disappear even if it should mean that the American republic be split in two. How ominous, how alarming this break appears. Progress, as a result of it, may remain at a standstill for fifty years to come.

John Brown has torn the veil; the American question has now become as important as the European question. Let us unite more than ever in defence of our two most precious rights and sternest responsibilities: Freedom and Truth. The republican conscience is the conscience of all Humanity. France owes America the truth, for she is the elder sister. . . .

Excerpt from a letter to George Sand:

December 20, 1859

Today I feel sick at heart. They've just killed John Brown. The murder was committed on December 2nd. The reprieve they had supposedly granted him was simply an infamous maneuver to silence public indignation. And to think that all of that has taken place in a republican state! What sinister madness to be the owner of men—see where it leads to! Here is a free nation killing a liberator. I am sore at heart. The crimes of kings are one thing, they are in the logical order of things, but profoundly unbearable to the thinker are the crimes of a whole community. . . .

After the death of John Brown, Victor Hugo made his now famous drawing of the condemned man on the gallows. Paul Chenay, a well-known engraver and brother-in-law of Hugo's, expressed a wish to engrave and publish this drawing. Here follows an excerpt from Hugo's letter to Chenay.

January 21, 1861

John Brown is a hero and martyr. His death was a crime—his gallows a cross. You'll recall that I wrote beneath my drawing *Pro Christo, sicut Christus.* In December of 1859 when I sorrowfully predicted the breaking apart of the Union as a direct result of the murder of John Brown, I did not expect the event to follow so closely upon my words. All the significance of J.B.'s gallows has come to light now. . . . The dissolution of the Union, a great evil, and the abolition of slavery, an immense step forward, may now be considered accomplished facts.

As a lesson, let us place before all the Charles Town gallows, starting point of these momentous events. The whole value of my drawing, which you so graphically and faithfully produced with your remarkable talent, lies in the name of John Brown. . . .

COMPLETE WORKS OF VICTOR HUGO

THERE IS NO SUCH THING
AS DISTANCE TODAY

Count Agénor de Gasparin was elected
a member of the French Chamber of
Deputies in 1842. From then on, in
and out of office, he traveled extensively and, as an influential writer and
political figure, crusaded for the abolition of slavery. His book, a translation
of which was published in New York
in 1862, discloses his deeply felt re-
vulsion toward slavery as well as his
brilliantly perceptive analysis of Europe's role in the American war.

The real center of the American question is to be
found now in Europe; it is at Paris and London, not
at Washington and Richmond that the essential reso-
lutions are taken on which depend the future of the
United States. This is a serious reason that we should
watch over ourselves, for our responsibility here is
immense. I shudder when I think with what lightness
we amuse ourselves by carving up America. There
will be two Confederacies, or rather three—that of
the North, the South and the West! Such are the
speeches that we carelessly throw out! How do we

know that our enthusiasms may not become weapons in the hands of the champions of slavery, in the hands of the enemies of all the causes that we hold most dear!

In speaking of Europe, without particularizing France and England, I gain the advantage of warding off many complicated and actually insoluble questions. I need no longer ask whether it has been England or France that has sought to ensure the triumph of a system having the recognition of the South for its end and the inefficiency of the blockade for its means. We accuse the English; the English accuse us in turn. I prefer to believe till proofs are furnished to the contrary, that neither is right. It seems to me that public opinion has had a great share in the evil with which governments are unjustly charged. The real criminals, once again, are ourselves, the whole world, European ideas, which, instead of openly taking the part of the North, have let themselves be persuaded to adopt the theories of Charleston, and to proclaim the secession of the Slave States as lawful, beneficial and final.

To speak only of our material interests, the civil war which is desolating America, is ruining the cotton production and calling forth sufferings in our Old World which will go on increasing. If the South had known in advance that it could not count on us, it is not probable that it would have attempted an insurrection. Its plan is to secure time for Europe to intervene. Europe needs its cotton. Europe is at its mercy. Europe is about to aid and recognize it, Europe will seize on the first pretext that offers; she will break the blockade and impose peace. Take away these convictions from the South and you will cause the weapons to fall from their hands.

11

Do those who speak in ironical terms of calico and cotton forget that behind cotton are men, women and children—miseries already great, and which will go on increasing? Do they comprehend the significance of the words—deficiency of raw material, restrictions of markets, stoppage of manufactories, discharge of workmen, diminution of wages? As for me, I hope that the feeling of the rights of the Negro will never make me close my eyes to the sufferings of the white men. These sufferings, I may say, have not ceased to weigh for a year past upon my saddened imagination, and not the least evil, in my eyes, of the attitude adopted by Europe, is that of having prolonged the manufacturing and commercial crisis by avoiding to discourage the rebellion. . . .

One would have said that Europe leaped with joy at the thought of rending the United States in twain. From the first moment she seemed to cling to this idea and to be unwilling to renounce it. That the scheme may perhaps be realized, I have no wish to deny. There are some minds, enlightened in all else, upon which America produces the effect of a nightmare; they ask to be rid of it at any price; what wounds them in it is not only the real and serious evil which appears therein under various forms, but also, and perhaps chiefly, the good, the brilliant, the superior side of the United States. . . .

The policy recommended by the friends of the South is nothing less, let us not forget, than the rule of Europe in America, by which I do not mean any mingling of Europe in American discussion. No, I am not one of those who believe that the Monroe Doctrine would remain intact amidst the conflicts of the nineteenth century. I believe in the frequent intervention of Europe in America and of America in

Europe; I believe in the future entrance of the United States into the concert of great powers; I believe, in fine, that electricity and steam have overthrown many artificial distinctions, and that it will daily become more difficult to live in isolation. But I believe at the same time that there should be neither European supremacy in America nor American supremacy in Europe. Nations are no longer in a state of pupilage, and pretensions of preponderance will soon cease to be tolerated anywhere.

The United States, it is exclaimed, will some day pretend to meddle in the affairs of the Old World, and to figure in the concert of great powers! Well, if this should be, what reason would we have to put on mourning? There is no such thing as distance today; and since Europe meddles with America, America may meddle with Europe. The solidarity of interests is real; is there a principle in opposition to that manifested by facts? Is it quite sure that the concert of great powers was completed in ten or twenty years, beyond the possibility of introducing the United States therein? Ought policy to live by fictions, or to seek realities?

What an immense step America has just taken! Between the presidency of Mr. Buchanan and that of Mr. Lincoln, there is the distance of social revolution. The sons of the Puritans are slow to move; but once set in motion, they go forward and nothing stops them.

Count Agénor de Gasparin, AMERICA BEFORE EUROPE

THE SIGNAL HAS BEEN GIVEN

Political exiles from Germany, Karl Marx and Frederick Engels settled in London in 1850. With income from his father's textile business, Engels helped support his friend. Marx became English correspondent for Horace Greeley's *Tribune* and served in that capacity more than ten years until early in 1862 he was told by the editor, Charles Dana, that American affairs would be taking up all the space in the paper. Marx and Engels collaborated in the *Communist Manifesto* (1848), the organization of the First and Second Internationals, and Engels brought *Das Kapital* to completion after Marx's death in 1883. During their long association a voluminous correspondence was carried on between the two men, which continued throughout and after the war years. Their letters give a panoramic picture of the Civil War as it unfolded and the authors' interpretations of the historical and revolutionary significance of the war. Further selections from their correspondence appear chronologically in this book.

Marx to Engels:

January 11, 1860

In my opinion, the biggest things that are happening in the world today are on the one hand the movement of the slaves in America started by the death of John Brown, and on the other the movement of the serfs in Russia. . . .

I have just seen in the *Tribune* that there has been a fresh rising of slaves in Missouri, naturally suppressed. But the signal has now been given. If things get serious by and by, what will then become of Manchester?

Marx and Engels, THE CIVIL WAR IN THE UNITED STATES

DOMESTIC GOSSIP TO PEOPLE
ENJOYING A REVOLUTION

William Makepeace Thackeray had already achieved major rank as a novelist with his *Vanity Fair* and *Henry Esmond* when he made his first visit to the United States as a lecturer in 1852–1853. His novel, *The Virginians,* contains material based on his second lecture tour in this country in the mid–1850's. Among his many American friends were Mr. and Mrs. George Baxter and their four children, a New York family with whom he maintained a close and regular correspondence after his return to England. At the outbreak of war Mr. Baxter was the prosperous owner of a warehouse in New York; his daughter Sally was married and living in the South while another daughter, Lucy (Libby), was married and living in the North. The following are excerpts of letters from Thackeray to the Baxters.

36 Onslow Square, Brompton
Christmas 1860

. . . I have been quill-driving all the morning, but I must say a word of God bless you to my dear kind friends at Brown House Street and wish you a Christmas as merry as may be. Aren't you in a fright at the separation? Is Sally going to be a countrywoman of yours no longer, and will her children in arms fight Libby's? It's a horrible thing to me to read of. . . . Is it this horrid Separation that has prevented your all coming to Europe? Or are you waiting till next year when my fine new house will be built?

To Mrs. Baxter:

This is not nice to tell is it? To write twopenny news of domestic gossip to people enjoying a revolution. I have never got to believe in it as serious as yet: and my impression of the U.S. is so incurably friendly that I can't fancy you quarrelling and hating each other. I cant think the fight will be a serious fight. In what will it benefit the North to be recoupled to the South? In the old wars we used to talk of the ruin of England as ensuing on the Separation of the Colonies . . . and aren't both better for the Separation? . . .

My dear friends:

I am glad to have a word of news of all of you, and that you should have wished to hear of me. I didn't write though I have thought of you many a time; and feared for you, lest the war should have brought its calamity down upon you. Before that grief wh I know must be in your house: what to say or to do? I know what your feelings are: loyal Northerns though you may be, with the daughter and grand-children in the South who look at us out of our photograph book so innocent & pretty and then there's the breadwinner, the warehouse. . . . does the warehouse bring any rent now? I know & feel that trying times are come to you all. . . . Now tell me my dear kind good Baxter and wife . . . there may be troubles at home—no dividends—the deuce to pay. I know a fellow who is not rich, for he has spent all his money in building this fine house: all but a very little—but who knows? Draw on me for 500£ at 3 months after date: and I am your man. You won't be angry? You may be worth millions and laugh at my impudence. . . . I dont know, but I dont mean no harm.

Affectionately yours,
WMT

Gordon N. Ray, LETTERS AND PRIVATE PAPERS OF WILLIAM
MAKEPEACE THACKERAY

"I DO NOT SEE HOW

THE UNITED STATES CAN BE

COBBLED TOGETHER AGAIN"

Lord John Russell left his mark on British parliamentary history as a liberal reformer. He served as Prime Minister from 1846–1852, with Palmerston as his Foreign Secretary. Their positions were reversed when Palmerston became Prime Minister, 1859–1865, and during those Civil

18

War years Russell consistently advocated neutrality. Upon Palmerston's death in 1865 Russell became Prime Minister again. The following are excerpts from his letters to Lord Lyons, the British Ambassador to Washington.

December 26, 1860

Do not seem to favour one party rather than the other . . . nor express opinions or give advice, unless asked for by the State Governments, in which case the advice should be against all violent action as tending toward civil war.

January 10, 1861

I do not see how the United States can be cobbled together again by any compromise. . . . I cannot see any mode of reconciling such parties as these. The best thing *now* would be that the right to secede should be acknowledged. . . . I hope sensible men will take this view. . . . But, above all, I hope no force will be used.

February 16, 1861

Above all things, endeavour to prevent a blockade of the Southern coast. It would produce misery, discord and enmity incalculable. . . .

19

I rely upon your wisdom, patience and prudence to steer us through the dangers of this crisis. If it can possibly be helped Mr. Seward must not be allowed to get us into a quarrel. I shall see the Southerners when they come but not officially, and keep them at a proper distance.

E. D. Adams, GREAT BRITAIN AND THE AMERICAN CIVIL WAR

A RUSSIAN OBSERVATION

Letter from Baron de Brunow, Russian Ambassador to England, to Prince Gortchakov, Russian Foreign Minister, January 1, 1861:

The English Government, at the bottom of its heart, desires the separation of North America into two republics, which will watch each other jealously and counterbalance one the other. Then England, on terms of peace and commerce with both, would have nothing to fear from either; for she would dominate them, restraining them by their rival ambitions.

E. D. Adams, GREAT BRITAIN AND THE AMERICAN CIVIL WAR

A BRITISH VIEW
OF AMERICAN ARISTOCRACY

The Confederate cause had its chief foreign support among the English aristocracy, the wealthy mill owners and shipbuilders. An organization representing these groups was formed in 1863 calling itself the Southern Independence Association. The Marquess of Lothian, one of the founders of the Association, naturally supported the South but so intuitive and ingrained was his sense of class distinction that he could not contain his snobbery even when speaking in behalf of his American counterparts.

I believe that the right of secession is so clear, that if the South had wished to do so for no better reason than that it could not bear to be beaten in an election, like a sulky schoolboy out of temper at not winning a game, and had submitted the question of its right to withdraw from the Union to the decision of any court of law in Europe, she would have carried her point.

But there are arguments to fall back upon in favor

of the North when this one about the illegality of secession falls through; they are, I fancy, principally three: 1. The United States Government is the best in the world. 2. The secession is a rebellion on the part of aristocrats against democracy; and this is a pet argument with Mr. Bright, upon whom the bare idea of an aristocrat, even when removed from him by the whole width of the Atlantic, operates like a red rag upon a bull. 3. Slavery is a dreadful thing; and this cry is echoed with vociferous irrelevancy by hundreds of voices, the leader of it being our present Foreign Secretary.

I fancy that there is in some of the Southern States what may be called an approach to an aristocratic class; that is, a class of men who hold the same land as their grandfathers held and can pretend to something like a pedigree. If anyone thinks that a reproach he is welcome to do so.

It would be a mistake to say that there is no such thing as an aristocracy in the United States. It is one, it is true, which those of Sparta, Rome, or Venice might not have been particularly anxious to acknowledge as akin to themselves, for its members lay no claim to character or statesmanship, and would repudiate the imputation of being gentlemen. But if a class of men, hereditary or not, succeeds in getting the government into its own hands and keeping the people out of it, such a class is fairly entitled to the name, even though its members be under-bred, low-minded jobbers. Such an aristocracy is the class of President-makers whom I have spoken of; and they bear rule not in the South but in the North.

It may very well be that hereditary wealth, by affording room for education, leisure, habits of command and independence, may point out those who possess it as fittest for that purpose; but it nowhere confers the right of nomination. And yet the people among whom this system prevails are called aristocrats by those who are themselves the helpless puppets of the irresponsible wirepullers of the North. The truth is, that the South has been getting more and more democratic. . . .

When one considers that slavery is a thing which has existed ever since the foundation of the world—that though it has often been considered as a *crime* —one is tempted to doubt whether all the indignation which one hears at the present day directed against slavery is not really directed against something else. . . .

And why, O ye haters of slavery! did you not speak out against the war of ten years ago? And you, ye fiery Radicals, supporters of the rights of man and all the rest of it! Have you not been praising America and American institutions to us all this time and alleging we ought to imitate them? And was not slavery one of those institutions? What did you say of the novels that made such a sensation some time ago? Were they not exaggerated, uncharitable, and everything else that was bad? Did you join in the general cry of indignation against the prototypes of Legree? Oh, no! We must not say a word against slavery; we must not hurt the feelings of our American brethern; they will find out in course of time that slavery does not pay, and then they will give it up; violent language will only exasperate them and irritate them into keeping it on. But how comes it that, after being so mealy-mouthed towards the Southerners when they were thought to be unmitigated ruffians, or at least selfish debauchees, your anti-slavery valour begins to find vent when they have unexpectedly developed the highest qualities that were ever displayed by any nation, and at the same time are struggling in a deadly grapple for everything which, either in the Old World or the New, is held most dear, against an adversary of overpowering strength? Has not the struggle shown that, however bad slavery might be in itself, it at any rate is not the monstrous tyranny and oppression in practice that we believed it to be? Is this your justice? Is this your generosity? Is this your sympathy with struggling nations? Can it be that you cannot forgive the Confederates for having taken away the point of your hustings speeches, in which you used to dilate upon the perfection of the model Republic, and prove how much better things were managed there than here, or would have a chance of being, unless your pet nostrums were applied to our constitution?

Marquess of Lothian, THE CONFEDERATE SECESSION

SLAVERY CORRUPTS THE SOUL

Elysèe Reclus, distinguished French geographer and writer, was the author of a remarkable *Géographie Universelle*. Because of his political opinions he was obliged to leave France after the coup d'état of 1851 and spent several years traveling in England, the

United States and South America. Upon his return to France in 1857, he became a regular contributor to the *Revue des Deux Mondes,* his brilliantly written articles being exclusively devoted to the cause of emancipation. His opinions were considered so influential in keeping France from intervention in favor of the South that the American minister to France, William Dayton, reportedly offered Reclus a large sum of money, which the young geographer refused. The pieces which follow are excerpts from articles dated December 15, 1860, and January 1, 1861.

Physical suffering and illness are nothing, though, compared to moral debasement for they concern only the body. But degradation of the soul corrupts the entire slave population, rots to the core not only the present generation but generations yet unborn; it poisons the race itself and justifies the oppressors in their own eyes by fitting the slave for slavery. The Negro who is flogged suffers more severely in his soul than in his body. He is ashamed of himself, dares not lift his eyes to the man who beats him or to those who have overheard his screams of pain, or even to his own children who witnessed his punishment. He despises himself and others as well, and his only respect is for the whip which holds him in check. If he dares to hate his master his hatred will be of a brutal, envious, groveling nature; his only weapon will be cunning and deceit, his only joys, coarse physical sensations. The Negro who has the courage to regard his master with calm scorn and feel superior to him because he has not committed the crime of buying and selling his fellow man is rare indeed. This crushing of simple, honest pride, this annihilation of all moral and intellectual life are the supreme expedient—the surest way to achieve through the disgrace of slavery a kind of animal delight.

What gives the slaveholders such formidable strength is neither their powerful solidarity nor the frightening audacity with which they face the hazards of the slave trade. Nor is it the cowardice or the ignorance of their Negroes. It is rather the indifference to their northern foe. All over the world people believe that the abolitionists' only aim is to achieve the emancipation of the Negro. But this, unfortunately, is not at all the case. The majority among them demand the abolition of slavery simply to prevent the white man from competing with servile labor. Hatred it is and not love of the black race that determines their attitude toward emancipation. But there are men filled with courage and heroic resolution who claim as brothers these black-skinned slaves. Garrison, the undaunted printer . . . Thomas Garrett, the heroic Quaker who provided more than two thousand slaves with a hiding place and helped them on to the road to freedom . . . John Brown and his companions who fought nobly and died more nobly still . . . a woman too, Mrs. Harriet Beecher Stowe, who awakened the interest of the whole world in the cause of the oppressed Negro—all these brave and selfless men and women have become more and more numerous in the last few years.

Unfortunately, there are still not enough of them to form a real party. Those who are now undertaking the electoral crusade against slavery and who hold in their hands the destinies of the whole republic are generally inspired by motives having very little to do with abnegation and justice. . . . They are quick to speak in terms of justice and liberty but it cannot be said that they have made any effort in their own states to raise the Negroes to their own level, either morally or materially. Preachers in their New England pulpits inveigh against the sin of slavery, poets stigmatize the ignoble slave merchants in inflammatory verses, ladies hold meetings to read abolitionist pamphlets and workers assemble from time to time to wrest a runaway slave from the hands of his persecutors. But all of these zealous defenders of their Negro brothers enslaved in distant plantations seem to forget the very existence of some of those black-skinned brothers of theirs who happen to be living right beside them. They love and cherish only those Negroes who have the wit to live south of the 36 degree of latitude.

Elysèe Reclus, REVUE DES DEUX MONDES

THE "TIMES" GOES SOUTH

London, January 9, 1861—The southern people—a proud, lazy, excitable and violent class, ever ready with the knife and the revolver. . . . We cannot disguise from ourselves that there is a right and wrong in this question, and that the right belongs to the States of the North. The North is for freedom of discussion and the South resists freedom of discussion with the tar brush and the pine faggot. . . . South Carolina has as much right to secede from the nation called the United States as Lancashire from England. . . . The Southern States expected sympathy for their undertaking from the public opinion of this country. The tone of the press has already done much to undeceive them.

London, May 28, 1861—The southern aristocracy— gentlemen, well-bred, courteous and hospitable. . . . A genuine aristocracy who have time to cultivate their minds, to apply themselves to politics and the guidance of public affairs . . . who travel and read, love field sports, racing, shooting, hunting and fishing, are bold horsemen and good shots. . . . Neither side can claim superiority of principle. The question is simply whether the ten millions of the Southerners shall become independent according to their desires or the twenty millions of Northerners remain powerful according to their desires.

NOTES FROM THE BELGIAN PRESS

By Special Correspondent from New York, January 10, 1861—Consumatum est! South Carolina has just separated itself from the United States. The scattering of the pearls from the necklace has begun.

It is much to be regretted that some of the southern states disregard in the haughtiest manner any taking into account of the predictions of the European press, if only to make emphatic denials. The "Grand Mogul" of journalism, the London *Times,* was particularly unfortunate in its appreciation of the political situation. One should also see how our newspapers cheer themselves with the prophecies of the Great Thunderer.

There shall not be a rupture of federal ties no matter what the correspondent of the *Independance* says. Here is South Carolina separating herself bravely —a little crazily—from the American Union. Bah! Europe will again say, it's only one state less than thirty-three; there will be no imitators. Well, another three weeks and Georgia, Alabama, Mississippi, perhaps Florida, even Louisiana will make common cause with South Carolina. The Union will break and break hard. It is certainly a great misfortune, but when the victorious party does not wish to make any concessions to the defeated party, when the *Tribune* and other newspapers each day pour out torrents of sarcasm, insults and threats—is it then so surprising that the Party of Moderation which struggles so bravely in Congress recognizes the uselessness of its efforts and is giving up the fight?

Let no one be misled by my thoughts. I have the most violent hatred for slavery that could be aroused in a disciple of Wilberforce. But why, because the chimney is smoking, is it necessary to burn the house?

L' INDEPENDANCE BELGE

THE UNITED STATES
CAN NEVER EXIST AGAIN

A man of great wealth, Alexander J. Beresford-Hope began his parliamentary career as an uncompromising conservative and retained that position to the end of his days. Hope's devotion to the Church of England was so great that he established a college for missionary clergy in Canterbury. He was a frequent contributor to the *Morning Chronicle* on religious matters and eventually Hope, with John Douglas Cook, the editor of the *Chronicle,* founded the *Saturday Review.* In 1861 Hope gave three lectures on the Civil War which he later printed. The following excerpt from one of these published lectures reveals the ludicrous distortions and blind prejudices of the class for which he was a leading spokesman.

I am sure that no assembly of Englishmen ever hears slavery mentioned without feeling the deepest aversion to it, but we ought to put the saddle upon the right horse. It is right we should remember that the Southern States inherited slavery from the old British colonial days—that many men in the North wish to see it abolished—that however wasteful of labour, however demoralising, it is not so generally cruel as many believe. People's idea of slavery is for the most part derived from Mrs. Stowe's novels. She is no doubt a clever writer, but she is the mouthpiece of the ultra-abolitionist party. Slavery is a curse and a misfortune to the country in which it exists, but the best of the slaveowners makes its chains as light as possible—they educate their blacks, they make them Christians, while in Africa they would have remained untaught and uncivilised.

The North contains a large population, enormous wealth, cities growing up like mushrooms, great literary activity, great scientific inquiry, great display of education, great facilities of locomotion, great manufactories, everything, in a word, tending to civilisation in an outside and selfish sense. . . . There are many excellent men in the country, men whose thorough English hearts bespeak their ancestry, but where are they politically? The educated and the rich are at a perfect disadvantage. Universal suffrage tramples everything down to a dead level. Infidelity is rampant, there is the grossest superstition, spirit-rapping, and so forth. Habitual divorce saps the foundations of domestic life. . . .

We now come to the events which heralded the present struggle. . . . Eighteen-sixty brought with it another Presidential election. The Republicans met at Chicago to nominate their candidate. At this Chicago Republican Convention there was a tall attorney, named Lincoln, a man brought up in a rough way, a clever woodcutter, one who could navigate a barge

31

down the Mississippi better than most men, and more especially famous as a rail-splitter, it being recorded that on one occasion he took a contract to split 30,000 rails in a marvellously short space of time. He could talk glibly enough, and managed to get elected a member of the Illinois House of Representatives, an assembly not quite so polished as the English House of Commons. We then find him figuring as an attorney at the county town of Springfield, and in 1847 he was elected a member of the House of Representatives at Washington. In 1849 Mr. Lincoln's Parliamentary career at Washington ended, but he was a great man down in Illinois. The consequence was that . . . when they met to select a candidate to be the future ruler for four years of thirty millions of the Anglo-Saxon race at a most trying period of history, they nominated the famous bargee, rail-splitter, and attorney, Abraham Lincoln, who, last autumn, was elected President of the United States. I dare say nobody in this country, clever as he might be at rail-splitting, at navigating a barge, or at an attorney's desk, would, with no other qualifications, ever become Prime Minister of England, let alone County Court Judge. . . .

The Republicans, in triumph of their success, were very sweet-mouthed, but it was well known that now they had got the curb rein in their hand they would grind down the Southern States beneath a crushing despotism. The South was placed in a position such as no great district had been placed before under the form of constitutional freedom—it was to be ruled over its entire wide area by the man whom it had with one voice rejected. . . . The first move was made by the fiery State of South Carolina, which voted itself straight out of the Union. . . . Six other States, Georgia, Alabama, Florida, Mississippi, Louisiana, and, later, Texas, soon followed. . . . They then proceeded to the election of a provisional President, and their choice fell upon a man who had stood out as the leader of opinion in the South, one who would never have been elected President of the United States, simply because he was a man of commanding intellect, but whom the Montgomery Congress, from some inscrutable reason, put at the head of affairs in the South. This man was Jefferson Davis. . . . Without relying too much on physiognomy, I appeal to the *carte de visites* of both Lincoln and Davis, and I think all who see them will agree that Jefferson Davis bears out one's idea of what an able administrator and a calm statesman should look like better than Abraham Lincoln, great as he may be as rail-splitter, bargee, and country attorney.

In April, when Lincoln had been President for a month, with Seward as his Secretary of State, it became known that a small fort in the harbour of Charleston, the principal town of South Carolina, still held by a Major Anderson for the North, was being quietly reinforced from Washington, when the South Carolinian armament, under the command of an able officer named Beauregard, attacked Fort Sumter, and after a sharp conflict, in which, however, no man fell on either side, succeeded in capturing it. . . . It is, by the way, a singular thing that most of the principal officers both in the army and navy of the United States should have sided with the South. . . . In fact, nearly all the chief men in both services joined the cause of Dixie Land, as the South is pleased to call itself, after a favourite Negro melody in honour of a model planter of old times, imaginary or real, called Dixie; while the New Englanders, and in a measure all the North are called Yankees. . . .

The fall of Fort Sumter caused one of those sudden

33

and shameless changes of feeling in the North to which democracies are most prone. Up to that time the secession had been more than excused. The loss of that stronghold irritated the national vanity, and hanging was too good for the rebels. Lincoln and his Prime Minister, Mr. Seward, veered with the wind and shouted war. Every State in the North turned out its mobs with new-made colonels and captains, self-elected, fresh from the shopboard or worse, and called them regiments of volunteers. These trooped in shoals to Washington. . . . England, of course, followed by France, issued a proclamation of neutrality as between the "belligerents." Seward, speaking through the ribald press of New York, took advantage of this political and necessary step to bespatter England with an unceasing torrent of calumny and vituperation, which has not yet ceased, while France, which had taken the same course, was prudently let alone. At the same time they sent their ships to blockade a country which they refused to acknowledge as belligerent, and called on foreign countries to acknowledge that blockade.

Thus did the North engage upon a war for domination in which spite, vanity, and the lust of uncontrolled supremacy were the main agencies. The most businesslike step which the North took was to establish their blockade of the Southern ports. The South, on its side, is holding its cotton crop inland, as a measure of precaution for fear of seizure, and as the basis of their war currency, ready to be let loose on the world as soon as peace comes and the Confederate States are admitted among the family of nations.

The North seems deluded with the idea that if the South were once subdued it would be easy to reconstruct the Union. We who live at a distance, and can

34

look at these things impartially, know how utterly impossible it is that the United States can ever exist again. No doubt the South is greatly in want of money. . . . Nevertheless they raise armies and equip them, we hardly know how. . . .

It was at one time fancied that slavery would be an element of weakness to the South, but so far from the slaves rising in a servile insurrection, they are actually a right arm of strength to their owners, and much as we may wonder at it, they seem to be working hard for the very men against whom it was supposed they would be the first to turn their hands. For the snubbing which the President gave Fremont in the matter of his proclamation declaring the immediate emancipation of slaves I praise Lincoln, for the horrors of war would be increased a thousand fold were a servile rebellion fostered.

But what will be the end of the struggle? One thing appears perfectly certain—the North cannot conquer the South. They may devastate it, they may sacrifice millions of treasure and a host of men, but they will never permanently subjugate the South against its will. If we look at the map with impartial eyes, we must rise convinced that the country should be divided into at least four great commonwealths, the North West, the Midland, the South, and the Pacific. Once divided into a number of commonwealths, each would be a check upon the other, and each would fall into the position of an European nation. Each would have to maintain its frontier, to keep up a standing army, to have a watchful Foreign Office. Every other country in the world does the like, and it is time that our bumptious cousins, now that they have become men and acquired bone and sinew, should assume the responsibilities of life and no longer display that

35

childish petulance which may have been excusable in the young days of the Republic.

We cannot help seeing that the North, with all its civilization, is the hotbed of anarchy, and that the South, in spite of the dark blot which stains its escutcheon, is fighting with one heart and mind for its independence from a hateful thraldom. We cannot help seeing that, while Abraham Lincoln is an incapable pretender, Jefferson Davis is a bold, a daring, yet politic statesman. We may well wish to see the American States peacefully separate into the great divisions marked out by Nature—we may well wish to see bloodshed cease and peace restored; but I contend, and I know the majority of thinking men in this country agree with me, though they are too mealy-mouthed as yet to say so, that the best and readiest method towards that end will be the establishment, as soon as possible, of the complete independence of the Confederate States.

Alexander J. Beresford-Hope, A POPULAR VIEW OF THE
AMERICAN CIVIL WAR

"PUNCH" AND THE "TIMES" ON COTTON

March 30, 1861—

Though with the North we sympathise
It must not be forgotten

That with the South we've stronger ties
Which are composed of cotton.

PUNCH

London, April 29, 1861—So nearly are our interests intertwined with America that civil war in the United States means destitution in Lancashire.

THE TIMES

May 27, 1861—"The republican bubble has burst. . . ."

Sir John Ramsden, in the House of Commons

London, June 1, 1861—The destiny of the world hangs on a thread . . . never did so much depend upon a mere flock of down!

THE TIMES

"I HAD MANY REASONS
FOR DECLINING THE MISSION"

William Howard Russell joined the staff of the London *Times* in his early twenties. As foreign correspondent for that paper he covered the Danish-

Prussian War, the Crimean War and
the Sepoy Mutiny in India. Russell's
reports to the *Times* were so popular
that his name as a journalist, war correspondent and military expert became as well-known in America as in
Europe. In the following letter to his
friend John Bigelow, American Consul General to Paris and later Minister
to France, Russell explains why he
accepted the Civil War assignment
from the London *Times*. We shall
hear from this famous war correspondent again later in the book.

Early in February, 1861, I was asked by Mr. Delane,
the editor of the *Times,* if I could make arrangements to proceed immediately to the United States
to act as the special correspondent of that paper in
observing the rupture between the Southern States
and the rest of the Union, consequent upon the election of Mr. Lincoln and the advent of the Republicans to power. The letters of Mr. Bancroft Davis, the
Times' correspondent at New York, were not in accord with the views of Printing House Square. He
was an uncompromising Abolitionist; his correspondence was in direct antagonism to the *Times'* leaders.
"The South," wrote Mr. Delane, "threatens to secede,
but that has been held up as a menace for a long
time, and the quarrel will be patched up; for the
North cannot live without the South, and lives, indeed, a good deal on and by it," and so on for four
closely written pages of note-paper. I had many
reasons for declining the mission. My wife was in

delicate health, my children were growing up, and since 1854 I had been constantly in exile in the Crimea, Russia, India, and Italy. My life was at that time very pleasant. The Garrick Club then afforded the most agreeable society I could wish, for Thackeray, Dickens, Shirley Brooks, Millais, Trollope, Reade, and other delightful people less known to fame, as well as many of the soldiers I had met in the Crimea and India, were familiar friends there. But I was urged by the editor, to whom I was bound by a hundred good offices, to make a sacrifice and to put on harness once more for his sake. I felt I had few qualifications for the post. I was almost entirely ignorant of the nature of the crisis and of the issues at stake, though I had read *Uncle Tom's Cabin,* had attended abolition meetings at Stafford House, and read extracts from fiery speeches of Calhoun and other Southern orators in the London papers. I had a vague idea that the Southern States insisted on their right to break away from the Federal Union and set up on their own account if they liked, and that was all I knew. Mr. John Henry Dillon, an acquaintance of Mr. Mowbray Morris, the manager of the *Times,* and of Mr. Delane, to whom I was referred for further information, was an ardent partisan of the South. Mr. Dillon astounded me by arguments to prove that the authors of the Union had provided for its disintegration by the machinery of States' Rights; and, finally, he confided to me, as a precious arsenal containing arms for the destruction of Abolitionists and Republicans, an immense volume of articles, neatly pasted in order, from the New York *Herald.*

John Bigelow, RETROSPECTIONS OF AN ACTIVE LIFE

A RUSSIAN DIPLOMAT REPORTS

Until the outbreak of the war, Anglo-American rivalry had "been the best guarantee against the ambitious projects and political egotism of the Anglo-Saxon race." Thus wrote Baron Edouard de Stoeckl, Russian Ambassador at Washington, to Prince Gortchakov, Minister for Foreign Affairs at St. Petersburg. The Russians believed that Britain alone would benefit from an event which would be fatal to the rest of the world. By the fall of 1862 British and French intervention appeared really imminent and even Russia was mentioned in the general alarm. Prime Minister Gortchakov cooled the British and French Interventionist zeal in an article published in the *Journal de St. Petersbourg* in which he stated that, "Russia entertains for the United States of America a lively sympathy founded on sentiments of mutual friendship and on common interests. She considers their prosperity necessary to the general equilibrium. She is convinced that the American nation can only find in the preservation of the Union the conditions of power and prosperity which she wishes to see it enjoy." Baron de Stoeckl, the Russian representative at Washington whose correspondence with Prince Gortchakov follows here, spent about twenty years in Washington in various diplomatic capacities and during that time married an American woman, Elizabeth Howard. The excerpts cover the period from February, 1861, to the spring of 1865. The quotations from 1862 to the end of the war will be found in their chronological order in this book.

1861

There is no doubt that religion and humanity condemn slavery, but the government must have time to uproot so great an evil. To accomplish this end it is necessary to combine with intelligence adequate legal measures, proper timing, and a willingness to give up some private property rights. The number of slaves in the United States has increased to 4,000,000, representing a capital of more than three billion dollars, without counting the losses which would be suffered by those sections which would become impoverished by the freeing of the slaves, since whites cannot labor in the hot climate of the Mississippi valley and the coast of the Gulf of Mexico. The figures I have cited prove the impracticality of emancipating the slaves by indemnifying the slaveholders as England did in her colonies. Abolition of slavery will be accomplished only by a gradual process. . . .

Mr. Lincoln does not appear to possess the talents and the energy which his Party attributed to him when they nominated him as their candidate for the Presidency. Even his partisans admit today that he is a man of irreproachable honesty but of mediocre ability.

Without having a remarkable face, Mr. Lincoln has an agreeable and honest expression. His manners are those of a man who has spent all his life in a small Western town, but he was polite and engaging toward all, and in general the diplomatic corps has only praise for the reception which was given it. . . .

An army of from 200,000 to 250,000 men, they are untrained. The stagnation of business and industry threw thousands of persons onto the streets who found relief only in the army. The large cities furnished the vast majority of these men. They are a strange conglomeration of all nationalities. Several regiments are composed entirely of Germans. Others contain only Irish. There are still others in which you find Spaniards, Italians, Belgians and French. There are even a number of Russians and Serbians. The generals are men who only yesterday were lawyers and merchants, and are entirely ignorant even of the elementary principles of their new offices. Officers of the regiments are chosen by the soldiers, so how can they issue orders to men to whom they owe their positions and who have the right to dismiss them at will? Some 50,000 to 60,000 troops are bivouacking in the environs of Washington. It is difficult to name a form of disorder or rowdyism they do not commit, and under the very eyes of the President and the high command. Is it any wonder then that General Scott hesitates to undertake an invasion with an army composed of such elements, particularly with the season of bad weather approaching? . . . .

The more complicated the situation becomes the more feeble and undecided he [Lincoln] appears. He admits that his task is beyond his powers. Fatigue and anxiety have broken him down morally and physically. As for Mr. Seward, his services in the office of Secretary of State hardly justify the high reputation he formerly enjoyed. He is completely ignorant of international affairs. At the same time his vanity is so great that he will not listen to anyone's advice. His arrogance harms the administration more than does the mediocrity of his colleagues.

On the Battle of Bull Run:

At about 4 o'clock . . . General Beauregard hurled 2,000 cavalrymen, who had not up to this time taken part in the action, against the federal army. . . . The effect of this maneuver was instantaneous. All troops without exception took to their heels and soon the entire army was one mad stampede in the woods and on the highways. The officers of the militia were the first to take flight, and the soldiers ran after them, throwing away their haversacks and rifles. It was thus that the federal army returned to Washington only four days after taking to the field.

The brilliant maneuver of General Johnston and the bungling retreat of General Patterson can be explained by the fact that the former is one of the most capable officers of the army, whereas the latter is a Philadelphia stockbroker. He was stripped of his command, but apparently they have not profited from

43

their mistake, as they replaced him by Mr. Banks, a Boston lawyer.

The day after the battle, Washington offered a sad spectacle indeed. Groups of soldiers returned from the battlefield, exhausted and bedraggled, crowded the streets and begged for food from door to door. A deadly fear pervaded the city that momentarily it might be invaded. Fortunately, a thousand regular troops performing police functions succeeded in leading the deserters into the camps near the Capital which they had occupied prior to the march on Virginia, and order was restored. It is impossible to describe the confusion which the disaster has caused here. The administration and Congress have completely lost their heads. In the secret meetings being held here day and night no one listens, for confusion is everywhere. No one seems to possess authority to give directions for the future. . . .

It is sad to see a nation which was so prosperous hardly a year ago dragged toward its complete ruin by demagogues who have risen from the scum of the population, whose personal interest is their only guide—who risk everything, for they have nothing to lose. A contributing factor to the disorder which prevails everywhere in the administration, as in the army, is that everyone believes that he has the right to meddle in the affairs of state, or at least to give advice. There is not a newspaper which does not recommend its own military strategy and plans, and which does not have its favorite general whom it extols to the skies. Spinster ladies visit the hospitals and create embarrassment or annoyances, but every one of them wants to play the role of Miss Nightingale. Some committees named by charitable organizations go through the camps followed by doctors and

French cooks to teach the soldiers to take care of their health and to cook. Finally, religious sects, of which there is a considerable number here, send deputation after deputation to enjoin the President to observe the Sabbath strictly in the army.

Our personal position is hardly better. We have for a garrison a large undisciplined army of volunteers recruited for the most part from the dregs of the large cities. . . . More than once, I and my colleagues have been exposed to the excesses of these volunteers, but we have not complained formally in order not to embarrass the government which already has problems enough. Luckily the Potomac shelters us from sudden attack by the enemy whose advance posts are only 4 or 5 *versts* from here. But they can cross the river easily twenty-five miles from here and surprise the city from the rear. In such case I do not know from where we would be threatened most—from the soldiers who are here to protect us, or from the Confederates who may attack us. Probably we would be plundered by both. My wife, along with the families of all the diplomats, has gone North, and as for us we are so accustomed to these conditions that we don't think anything about them. . . . We are not far from a reign of terror such as existed during the great French Revolution, and what makes the resemblance more striking is that all these acts of oppression are made in the name of liberty.

Albert Woldman, LINCOLN AND THE RUSSIANS

TWO PRESIDENTS

AND A DISASTROUS ROUT

In the following three selections William Howard Russell describes the spoils system and its effect on President Lincoln, sketches a vivid picture of Jefferson Davis and asserts in a letter to John Bigelow that he has been wildly misquoted on his report of the Battle of Bull Run.

Washington, March 29, 1861—Willard's Hotel, a huge caravanserai, is a curious study of character and institutions. Every form of speech and every accent under which the English tongue can be recognized rings through the long corridors in tones of expostulation, anger or gratification. Crowds of long-limbed, nervous, eager-looking men, in loose black garments, undulating shirt collars, vast conceptions in hatting and booting, angular with documents and pregnant with demand, throng every avenue, in spite of the printed notices directing them "to move on from in front of the cigar-stand." They are "senator hunters," and every senator has a clientele more numerous than the most popular young Roman noble who ever sauntered down the via Sacra.

At the head of the list of persecuted men is the President himself. Every one has a right to walk into the White House, which is the President's private as well as his official residence. Mr. Lincoln is actuated by the highest motives in the distribution of office. All the vast patronage of tens of thousands of places, from the highest to the lowest, is his; and, instead of submitting the various claims to the heads of departments, the President seeks to investigate them, and to see all the candidates. Even his iron frame and robust constitution are affected by the process, which lasts all day and is not over in the night or in the morning. At the very moment when the President and his Cabinet should be left undisturbed to deal with the tremendous questions which have arisen for their action, the roar of office seekers dins every sense and almost annihilates them. This hunting after office . . . these "spoils," as they are called, are now being distributed by two Governments—the *de jure* and *de facto* Government of Washington, and the Government erected by the Southern States at Montgomery.

William Howard Russell, THE CIVIL WAR IN AMERICA

Montgomery, May 7, 1861—Today I proceeded to the Montgomery Downing Street and Whitehall to present myself to the members of the Cabinet and to be introduced to the President of the Confederate States of America. There is no sentry at the doors, and access is free to all. Mr. Davis is a man of slight, sinewy figure, rather over the middle height, and of erect, soldier-like bearing. He is about fifty-five years of age; his features are regular, but the face is thin and marked on cheek and brow with many wrinkles, and is rather careworn and haggard. One eye is apparently blind, the other is dark, piercing and intelligent. In the course of conversation he gave an order for the Secretary of War to furnish me with a letter as a kind of passport in case of my falling in with the soldiers of any military posts who might be indisposed to let me pass freely.

It is amusing to hear the tone used on both sides toward Great Britain. Both are most anxious for her countenance and support, although the North blusters rather more about its independence than the South, which professes a warm regard for the mother country.

William Howard Russell, THE CIVIL WAR IN AMERICA

After witnessing a slave auction the following day Mr. Russell describes his reactions in a letter to the *Times:*

Montgomery, May 8, 1861—I tried in vain to make myself familiar with the fact that I could, for the sum of $975, become as absolutely the owner of that mass of blood, bones and sinew, flesh and brains as of the horse which stood by my side. There was no sophistry which could persuade me the man was not a man— he was, indeed, by no means my brother, but assuredly he was a fellow creature. . . .

E. D. Adams, GREAT BRITAIN AND THE AMERICAN CIVIL WAR

The following letter refers to Russell's report of the Federal rout at Bull

Run, which evoked considerable controversy on both sides of the Atlantic:

Washington, July 27, 1861

My dear Bigelow:

It is not true that I commanded the Confederates in person or led off the Federalist centre; neither did I lie on my stomach disguised as Raymond of the *Times* and kill Beauregard with a pistol toothpick as he rode insultingly over the battle field; neither did I say that I had never seen such slaughter at Solferino (where I wasn't) or at Inkerman where I was; nor did I set down the loss of the Federalists at 12,000 (though I do think every way, it was near 1200); in fact anything you see in print about me, contradict point blank on my authority, even if it be that I am a gentleman who regards his word (for then I should begin to doubt it was so), or that I told any one anything in strict confidence, for then I am certain it is not true, and he would not print it correctly, in his anxiety to keep his trust. I don't mind telling you that a battle which should never have been fought at all, was hardly fought—*vu* the means to the end—was unsuccessful—and was terminated by the most singularly disgraceful panic and flight on record, with consequences of a more serious nature politically than were militarily evident. The attempt made to disguise the disasters of an army which left its guns and wagons (which could not be rallied at Centerville or even at Fairfax: "the wicked flee when no one pursueth") and fell upon Washington utterly routed by its own fears, must make the affair even more disastrous, because the smallness of the loss and the greatness of the actual result are withering commentaries on the monstrous mouthings about "unparalleled heroism" and the "orderly retreat" which appear in one of the papers. . . . I tell you I am satisfied from what I saw—particularly of the Penn. regiment which deserted the field on the day of battle *because time was up*—of the officers running from the field shouting out "we're whipped" and of the men who could not be held together, that the North will be beaten by the South as long as it relies on the present set of officers or of men. . . .

John Bigelow, RETROSPECTIONS OF AN ACTIVE LIFE

SIDE LIGHTS ON BULL RUN

Mowbray Morris, manager of the London *Times* in charge of foreign correspondents, wrote William Howard Russell on August 14, 1861:

When your description of the Bull's Run affair appeared in the *Times* everyone said, "Russell will be lynched," and there was very serious apprehension for your safety entertained even by men not usually given to idle fears.

In a letter written January 27, 1862, Russell told John Delane, editor-in-chief of the *Times*:

If I am ever in another Bull's Run you may depend on it I shall never get out of it alive. . . . It is a dead load around a man's neck to be feeling always that he is disliked and is liable to insult and outrage. I am the only English thing they can vent their anger on, and the *Times* is regarded as so dead against the North that everyone connected with it in the North is exposed to popular anger whilst I am especially obnoxious to it as I am supposed to be the cause of all the ill will of the paper to the Federal Gov't. It's hard work playing a neutral game unless you're on neutral ground, I can tell you. . . .

THE HISTORY OF THE LONDON TIMES

THESE ARMIES DIFFERED FROM OURS

The comte de Paris, a direct descendant in the line of Orleanist pretenders to the throne, came to America in 1861 with his brother, the duc de Chartres, and their uncle, the Prince de Joinville, and fought in the war under General McClellan. Eventually he became the head of the entire house of Bourbon. His four-volume *History of the Civil War in America* became a standard work of military history.

These armies differed from ours in the large number of married men they contained. In America there are no military laws to interfere with marriage, and the American, who is but little addicted to domestic habits and is the artificer of his own fortune, does not enter into those calculations concerning family expenses which stifle the spirit of enterprise in a nation, and eventually impoverish its population both morally and numerically. The war acted as a stimulus to marriage—among the officers, in the hope of being cared for by female hands if wounded; among the soldiers, because the States had assured a certain indemnity to their wives and a liberal pension to their widows. . . .

Vigor and skill among the volunteers did not exclude instruction. Active citizens in their respective counties and States, and identified with either of the political parties, they were fully acquainted with public affairs and could not dispense with newspapers. With scarcely any exception, they had all received that primary education which, without initiating the man into all the discoveries of science, teaches him to make use of his intelligence, which awakens a desire for knowledge, and which, when it pervades a whole population, imparts to it as much power as a simple unit placed before any number of zeros. It is owing to this general system of education that the New World may be called the country of progress, and that its institutions are founded upon the regular and conscientious practice of universal suffrage. The New England States are entirely exempt from those twin scourges inseparable from our old social systems, ignorance and pauperism. The illiterate minority of the army was almost exclusively composed of European emigrants.

On opening the knapsack of the American soldier one was almost sure to find in it a few books, and generally a Bible, which he read in the evening without hiding from his comrades. An inkstand, a piece of blotting-paper, some envelopes ornamented with monograms, badges, and portraits completed the assortment. He made, in fact, abundant use of the liberality of the government, which transported all his letters postage-free. A large carpet-bag hung up against the tent of the adjutant of each regiment, served as a letter-box; and a few hours of rest sufficing to fill it, it was often necessary to empty it twice a day. Consequently, the arrival and departure of the mail played a great part in camp-life. Together with the correspondence, the mail brought enormous packages of newspapers, which ragged boys, both on foot and on horseback, distributed in great haste, even to the remotest corners of the camp. They were frequently seen crying their papers on the very field of battle, and selling them to the wounded scarcely able to rise. In every tent the latest news brought by the *Herald* or the *Tribune* was read in the evening and eagerly discussed, while the soldier on duty, if he thought himself unobserved, walked up and down with his musket in one hand and his newspaper in the other.

The great journals were represented in each army corps by an accredited correspondent, whose duty it was to see everything, to take part in every expedition, and to allow no incident of the war to pass without reporting it. This staff comprised the greatest variety of characters and peculiarities of life. In its

53

ranks were writers of positive merit and men who, animated by a real passion for war, ended by exchanging the pen for the sword. The life which circumstances compelled these correspondents to lead exacted special qualities—tact, daring, and a great deal of assurance, a still greater amount of patience and robust health. When a secret was divulged, the first suspicions fell upon them. In consequence of a few lamentable indiscretions, the government exacted a promise from all those engaged in writing for the newspapers not to publish what it was important to conceal from the enemy. They were therefore obliged to distinguish, among all interesting facts they were the first to learn, such as could lawfully be communicated to the public. More than once they had to resort to stratagem in order to evade the order of some incensed general who had forbidden their stay among his troops. Under such circumstances, to become a close observer and an agreeable reporter, to be tolerated by the generals and welcomed by the subordinates, to know how to repay each item of information with a kind and flattering word, and in case of necessity to enforce respect through the redoubtable influence which is derived from the support of a great journal, certainly required, to say nothing of mental qualifications, a character at once sprightly and tempered. A private individual in the midst of a large army, having neither the shoulder-straps of the officer nor the musket of the soldier with which to influence others, or even to justify his presence there; obliged to share the dinner of one man or to ask a ration of forage for his horse from another; always on the watch not to miss the hour of departure, which the jealous mistrust of the chief of staff carefully kept from his knowledge; always

ready to throw his wallet upon his horse—a wallet
oftener empty than full; sleeping wherever he could,
behind a tent, in a wagon, or under a tree—the correspondent, worn out with fatigue, was obliged every
night, whilst all around were reposing near the ex-
piring camp-fires, to take out his pen and compose
upon his knees, by the light of a wretched lantern, a
letter capable of entertaining a public difficult to
please and greedy for sensations. Real danger frequently caused these hardy pioneers of the press to
share the glory of the soldiers.

Comte de Paris, HISTORY OF THE CIVIL WAR IN AMERICA

THE REPUBLIC OF SAN MARINO
CONFERS CITIZENSHIP ON
PRESIDENT LINCOLN

San Marino, 29th March 1861

Our Dear Sir:

It is a some while since the Republic of San Marino
wishes to make alliance with the United States of
America in that manner as it is possible between a
great potency and a very small country. As we think
not extention of territories but conformity of opinions to procure friendly relations, so we are sure you

55

will be glad to shake hands with a people who in its smallness and poverty can exhibit to you an antiquity from fourteen centuries of free government maintained among the many revolutions of the surrounding countries, and always respected even by the conqueror Napoleon 1st. As also we are instructed that we are known to you especially for the hystory of our Republic written by Mr. Jean de St. Hyppolite and dedicated to the President of the United States, so we have not taken the diplomatic whay, and we have written to you directly.

Now we must inform you that to give to Mr. Lincoln President of the United States of America a mark of its high consideration and sincere fraternity the Sovereing Counsel on our motion decreed in the sitting of 25th October ult. that the citizenship of the Republic of San Marino was conferred to their President pro-tempore; and we are very happy to send you the diploma of it.

We are aequainted from newspapers with political griefs, which you are now suffering; therefore we pray to God to grant you a peaceful solution of your questions. Nevertheless we hepe our letter will not reach you desagreable, and we shall anxiously expect an answer, which prove us your kind acceptance.

We have wished to write to you with our own hand, and in English, although we have but little knowledge and no practice in the language. We have done that to render ourselves most pleasing to you and in writing to entertain ourselves fraternally with you a more time.

We are truly

The Regent Captains
Gaetano Bellurri
also for his Companion absent

HATRED PREVAILED

Maurice Sand, son of George Sand and Baron Dudevant, was one of the party that accompanied Prince Napoleon on a tour of the United States and Canada in 1861. Sand published an account of his trip in the form of letters to his mother. This party of French visitors spent some time in New York and then continued on to Washington where they were received by Secretary Seward who arranged a meeting with the President. In the excerpt immediately following, Sand describes the interview with Lincoln. Later, the party crossed over to the Confederate lines where they were received by Southern officers who impressed them with their elegant manners and gallantry. While in Confederate territory, Sand heard and recorded some bitter views expressed by officers and men in the ranks.

. . . A few moments later a small door opened to let in a very tall gentleman, six feet tall, very lean, dressed entirely in black, holding in his big hairy hands a pair of white gloves which had never been worn and never would be worn. A long nose, a large mouth, small, gentle eyes, hollow cheeks and a beard trimmed in the American style—which would make Jove himself look vulgar—a long lock of hair combed across his forehead and hanging down on the other side like a weeping willow, a kindly expression not without subtlety—such is "Honest Abe." He came forward awkwardly, somewhat timidly, shook hands first with the Prince, then with each of us, and made some efforts to engage us in friendly conversation. "How long did it take you to come from Europe? . . . Have I the honor of speaking to Lucien Bonaparte's son? . . . How do you like America? . . . Isn't it awfully hot?" The worthy man, quite evidently, was filled with the best intentions. But neither in his speech nor in his manner was this symbol of freedom free. . . .

It has been said and printed in the North that the wounded Union soldiers had all been slaughtered, and that a church in which some fifteen thousand of these poor wretches and their surgeons had found refuge had been violated. The Southern soldiers are said to have shot at them through the window. The rebels categorically deny this. Instead, they charge the Federal soldiers with strange acts of treachery. According to them, an enemy regiment came right up to them under cover of an apocryphal flag to take them unawares and murder them. One thing is certainly true: the lack of uniform, or rather the fantastic variety of military costume of both armies and the similarity of their flags (the only difference being in the number of stars), was certainly the cause of tragic mistakes. Soldiers have been known to shoot their own comrades and to give themselves up to the enemy, whom they had mistaken for friends. All the confusion, the bitterness, the slanderous charges that go with civil war were to be found. . . .

We may note, sad as the fact may be, that among the belligerents, hatred prevailed over every other feeling. "We don't want to force our way into their territory, but we will not permit one single Yankee to set foot on our soil," I was told. "We would rather burn our cotton than let them profit by it in the future. . . . If we had the right to join the Union then we also have the right to secede from it," were remarks I heard again and again. "They know very well that without us their trade is ruined, for we produce the raw materials and we won't let ourselves be exploited any longer. We will fight a year, or two or even four if need be. We've already sacrificed our incomes and we won't hesitate to sacrifice our lives, but we don't want to have anything more to do with them. England and France need what we produce and we are ready to deliver the goods to them directly, without passing through Northern hands."

Another spokesman: "Who ever talks about freeing the slaves in this country? Nobody. It's only in Europe that you find people worrying about it. We are supposed to spend most of our time flogging our Negroes. That kind of story is spread deliberately by our Yankee enemy to discredit us in the eyes of foreigners. They're jealous of our wealth. Come and visit Carolina, Georgia, New Orleans, and you will see for yourself what good care we take of our Negroes. If one of them happens to fall sick, we do our best to get him well. They're well housed, well fed, never overworked and they desire nothing else of life. They're much happier than the settlers out west. They're happier with us than in the North, where they have freedom all right, the freedom to starve to death." If answering such impassioned people hadn't been so utterly useless, I would have told them that they refused to face the real problem—the existence of slavery.

Yes, yes, paternalistic lords of the whip, you give yourselves away. Had you the right to secede from the Union? That's a question to be discussed in an assembly of calm men and not settled by force. Did you simply wish to increase your profits by dealing with Europe directly? Then that was a question of trade which could not be solved in combat, for war is the ruin of all trade. You should have the courage to acknowledge that your only aim is to extend slavery to the rest of the Union and to annex Mexico and Cuba. Your whole problem is how to have man work for you and not pay him for his labors. That is the source of your profit, your wealth, your alleged right, sanctioned by political action but rejected and annulled by humanity. . . .

Sand talked with an infantryman who told him:

"I am a Frenchman. I came to America to work as a gardener, but what with this war going on there's nothing but laurels left to tend now. The whole country's a mess, but a man still has to eat. So I enrolled for two years, for the duration of the campaign. But it's not like the soldiers back home—these fellows can't even hold a gun properly. And the ones from the North are just as bad. Besides, they are not as brave as our men—nearly all of their dead are found lying shot in the back."

"What about the pay?"

"It's all right in the infantry, but in the cavalry more than a third of the men get nothing at all."

"Have you got any Negro soldiers?"

"Negroes, for heaven's sake! A fine mess that would be!"

"You despise Negroes then?"

"How can I help disliking them? They get no pay, work like dogs and seem perfectly satisfied being slaves. It makes you feel like beating them up. It's because of them that we are forced either to starve to death or to get ourselves shot."

In those few words, he had, it seemed to me, summed up very well the pitiful state of degradation of the slave, satisfied with his lot, and the tragedy of a free man, whom this monstrous competition has reduced to want.

Maurice Sand, SIX MILLE LIEUES À TOUTE VAPEUR

"IT IS OUT OF MY LINE"

One of Charles Darwin's early supporters in this country was Asa Gray, America's leading botanist. Gray was a professor of natural history at Harvard and the author of numerous works on the natural sciences. A warm friendship between the two men was sustained over the years by an exchange of letters dealing primarily with questions of a scientific nature. As the war progressed more and more in grim earnest their letters reflected the deep concern of both scientists. The following are excerpts from letters of Darwin to Gray.

Down, June 5 [1861]

My dear Gray,—

I never knew the newspapers so profoundly interesting. North America does not do England justice; I have not seen or heard of a soul who is not with the North. Some few, and I am one of them, even wish to God, though at the loss of millions of lives, that the North would proclaim a crusade against slavery. In the long run, a million horrid deaths would be amply repaid in the cause of humanity. What wonderful times we live in! Massachusetts seems to show noble enthusiasm. Great God! how I would like to see the greatest curse on earth—slavery—abolished! . . .

Ever yours,
C. Darwin.

Down, September 17 [1861?]

My dear Gray,—

I thank you sincerely for your very long and interesting letter, political and scientific, of August 27th and 29th, and Sept. 2nd, received this morning. I agree with much of what you say, and I hope to God we English are utterly wrong in doubting (1) whether the N. can conquer the S.; (2) whether the N. has many friends in the South, and (3) whether you noble men of Massachusetts are right in transferring your own good feelings to the men of Washington. Again I say I hope to God we are wrong in doubting on these points. It is number (3) which alone causes England not to be enthusiastic with you. What it may be in Lancashire I know not, but in S. England cotton has nothing whatever to do with our doubts. If abolition does follow with your victory, the whole world will look brighter in my eyes, and in many eyes. It would be a great gain even to stop the spread of slavery into the Territories; if that be possible without abolition, which I should have doubted. You ought not to wonder so much at England's coldness, when you recollect at the commencement of the war how many propositions were made to get things back to the old state with the old line latitude, but enough of this, all I can say is that Massachusetts and the adjoining States have the full sympathy of every good man I see; and this sympathy would be extended to the whole Federal States, if we could be persuaded that your feelings were at all common to them. But enough of this. It is out of my line, though I read every word of news, and formerly well studied Olmstead. . . .

Your unmerciful correspondent,
C. Darwin.

Francis Darwin, LIFE AND LETTERS OF CHARLES DARWIN

"SURELY THESE PEOPLE
ARE NOT SLAVES?"

Samuel Phillips Day, special correspondent for the conservative London *Morning Herald,* found much to his liking in the manners and mores of the South, including slavery. The social and political climate of the Confederacy, as described in his book, *Down South,* had his unqualified and enthusiastic approval.

On Sunday [June 8th, Ashville, Kentucky, 1861] I took a drive with some friends. Judge of my surprise, reader, when I found almost the entire Negro population abroad; some parading thoroughfares, and others riding about in carriages! They were dressed so showily and so finely, and appeared so happy and contented, that I was voluntarily forced to exclaim several times, "Surely these people are not *slaves?*" The response was, "Certainly they are."

Positively some of the women wore lace shawls and gold watches, and, as I then observed, "looked (only for their colour) like London duchesses going to a ball!" The men, too, were well attired—most of them in light clothes, and immaculate shirts and collars, ornamented with gold studs. I reflected for a moment on the condition of British agricultural labourers and London needlewomen—the contrast was too painful to dwell upon.

When I considered that these people had been removed from a state of barbarism in Africa, and had become semi-civilized and semi-Christianized in the South, the thought flashed across my mind that there was nothing so very wicked in slavery after all—that it possessed a *bright* side as well as a *dark* side—and that Mrs. Beecher Stowe, and persons of similar shades of opinion, having lent the charms of their imagination to depict the one, it were well if something should be said regarding the more agreeable aspects of the other.

I have heard Southerners frequently complain that the real causes of the disruption of the Union, and the consequent war, were not rightly understood in Europe; that the North by false assertion, had prejudiced the minds of foreigners against the Confederacy, while endeavouring to enlist sympathy for herself; and they only asked the "attentive" hearing of enlightened European nations. . . .

Maddened by opposition, and humiliated by defeat, the North is employing all her resources, both by land and sea, to reduce an independent people to subjection. Her attitude towards the South has been one of uniform, persistent and irreconcilable hostility. The contests between the two sections of the Union were invariably founded on political and economical considerations—they never involved a moral question. . . . This war commenced with tariffs, and waged with tariffs, till a better substitute was found in bullets. . . . Both England and France have, commercially, a vital interest in this struggle; and their armed interference has been suggested by political considerations of no inferior magnitude. I believe that the Confederate Government is, of itself, abundantly able to hold its own in the struggle; but without the interposition of the European Powers, this conflict must be a long, bloody, and disastrous one; involving not only the interests of the American continent, but crippling the industry and paralyzing the enterprize of the world.

I was strongly impressed with one startling anomaly painfully and constantly observable in the Northern States, viz., that notwithstanding the philanthropic regard alleged to be entertained for the Negro in that portion of America, he is infinitely worse and more indignantly used than in the South. The black man is loathed in the North, and treated much after the same manner as the ancient Jews were accustomed to treat people affected with leprosy.

Down South the slaves, so far as my experience serves, are treated with the utmost humanity and kindness. . . . Nor does the Negro groan under the weight of his chains. I never met with human beings so perfectly happy and contented; or so thoroughly unacquainted with the carking cares and anxieties of life. Freedom! it is but a name to them. What do beings of that class care for freedom, which would only have the effect of destroying their present happiness, by bringing their labour into competition with that of the white man?

Samuel Phillips Day, DOWN SOUTH

PRUSSIA IS DISTURBED BY THE CONFLICT

A letter from Baron de Schlenitz, Prussian Minister of Foreign Affairs, to Baron von Grabow, Prussian Minister at Washington:

Berlin, June 13, 1861

The hope, which until now we so willingly entertained, that the inchoate conflict between the government of the United States and sundry of the Southern States of the Union would be brought to an amicable settlement, is now, unhappily, in view of existing conditions, borne back to a far distance. . . .

The relations of close friendship which connect Prussia and the Government of the United States exist from the foundation of the Union. They have endured nearly a hundred years, never at any time disturbed by change or circumstances, nor in any wise impaired. . . .

At no time between the two powers has any collision of antagonistic interests found a foothold. The soaring flight which the internal prosperity of the Union has taken, extending its range from year to year by means of the bond of unity of the States thus

67

knit together, the commanding altitude which North America has attained abroad has been looked upon by Prussia not merely with no dissatisfaction but has rather been greeted by her with honest sympathy. . . .

DIPLOMATIC CORRESPONDENCE, 1862

A LITTLE-KNOWN MOMENT
IN HISTORY

Authorized by President Lincoln, an offer of a command in the Union forces was issued in 1861 to the Italian patriot Garibaldi. Although deeply involved in the turbulent affairs of his own country, he replied, setting forth his own conditions of acceptance. Thereafter a series of ambiguous letters was dispatched by Garibaldi to American foreign service officials stationed in Europe. On September 17, 1862, Theodore Canisius, United States Consul in Vienna, uninstructed and without authority, wrote the Italian liberator, suggesting that since he had failed to achieve his aims in Italy he might be interested in lending a hand in our struggle. The letter, which was made public, stirred up considerable commotion in Europe. The London *Times* commented: "In the light of recent events, it is not impossible that we may yet see Garibaldi crossing the Atlantic in the assumed character of an American Citizen and fighting for the subjugation of a nation struggling to be free." Canisius, pleased with himself, informed Secretary Seward of what he had done. The Secretary of State promptly notified Canisius that he was fired. Seward subsequently revoked the dismissal when Canisius protested that his wife and children would be thrown helpless onto the streets of Vienna because of an act he had committed in all good faith and loyalty to the Union cause. Garibaldi's correspondence in this affair follows.

To J. W. Quiggle, American Consul at Antwerp:

Caprera, June 27, 1861

My dear Friend:

The news given in the Journals that I am going to the United States is not exact. I have had and still have a great desire to go, but many causes prevent me.

If, however, in writing to your government, and they believe my service of some use, I would go to America, if I did not find myself occupied in the defense of my country.

Tell me, also, whether this agitation is the emancipation of Negroes or not.

I should be very happy to be your companion in a war in which I take part by duty as well as sympathy.

I kiss with affection the hand of your lady, and I am,

with gratitude, yours,
G. Garibaldi

To H. Sanford, United States Minister to Belgium:

August 31, 1861

Mr. Minister:

I should be very happy to be able to serve a country for which I have so much affection and of which I am an adoptive citizen, and if I do not reply affirmatively and immediately to the honorable proposition which your Government through your agency has made to me, it is because I do not feel entirely free, because of my duties toward Italy.

Nevertheless, if His Majesty King Victor Emmanuel believes he has no need of my services, then provided that the conditions upon which the American Government intends to accept me are these which your messenger has verbally indicated to me, you will have me immediately at your disposal.

I am delegating Colonel Trecchi to speak to the

King and to give me a reply which will be communicated to you at once.

I am with consideration,

Faithfully yours,
G. Garibaldi

To J. W. Quiggle, American Consul at Antwerp:

Caprera, September 10, 1861

Dear Sir:

I have seen Mr. Sanford and I am sorry to be obliged to say that I cannot at present go to the United States. I have no doubt of the triumph of the cause of the Union and that it will come quickly; but if the war should by evil chance continue in your country, I will overcome all the obstacles which hold me back, and will hasten to come to the defense of that people which is so dear to me.

G. Garibaldi

H. Nelson Gay, "LINCOLN'S OFFER OF A COMMAND TO GARIBALDI"

To His Excellency, General Garibaldi:

Turin, September 17, 1861

Your Excellency:

The Undersigned refugee Polish officers discharged at their own request from the Southern Army of

Italy, who have had the honor to serve under you, beg to ask your Excellency—in the event that your Excellency accepts the rank of Commander-in-Chief of the Army of the United States—to accord them the favor to follow your Excellency and to form a separate division in your Army—should your Excellency refuse this important honor, we beg you to take us under your protection and urge the Government of the United States to admit us into its military service. It will be our duty to be worthy of this great honor.

Please accept the expressions of our deep respect and sincere devotion with which we are your Excellency's

Very humble and devoted servants
(17 illegible signatures)

Howard R. Marraro, "LINCOLN'S OFFER OF A COMMAND TO
GARIBALDI"

Garibaldi to Theodore Canisius, United States Consul at Vienna:

Varignana, September 14, 1862

Sir: I am a prisoner and dangerously wounded, therefore it is impossible for me to dispose of myself.

I believe, however, that when my imprisonment shall cease, and my wound heal, the favorable opportunity shall have come in which I will be able to satisfy my desire to serve the great American republic, of which I am a citizen, and which to-day fights for the universal freedom.

I have the honor to be, very respectfully,

G. Garibaldi

DIPLOMATIC CORRESPONDENCE, 1863

To George P. Marsh, United States Minister to Italy:

Varignana, October 7, 1862

My dear Sir:

I am ill and shall remain so for some months, but I think continually of the disastrous war in America, my second country, to which I would gladly be of some use when recovered. I will go thither with my friends; and we will make an appeal to all the democrats of Europe to join us in fighting this Holy battle. But in this appeal it will be necessary to proclaim to them the principle which animates us—the enfranchisement of the slaves, the triumph of universal reason. Please confer with your Government on this subject and communicate to me your ideas in regard to it, through my friend Colonel Vecchi.

Believe me, meanwhile, affectionately yours,

G. Garibaldi

Howard R. Marraro, "LINCOLN'S OFFER OF A COMMAND TO GARIBALDI"

Apparently Garibaldi had nothing less in mind than becoming commander-in-chief when he submitted his terms of acceptance to Secretary Seward. Perhaps he was not entirely convinced that only the President could hold that rank. In any event, the foregoing inconclusive correspondence was never resumed. Garibaldi's convalescence was slow and meanwhile the situation in the United States improved steadily. The North developed some fine generals of its own and the need for Garibaldi's services no longer existed.

TWO COUNTRIES, PLACED AT THE EXTREMITIES OF TWO WORLDS

Letter from Prince Gortchakov, Russian Minister of Foreign Affairs, to Baron de Stoeckl, Russian Ambassador at Washington:

Sir:

... For more than eighty years that it has existed, the American Union owes its independence, its towering rise and its progress to the concord of its members, consecrated under the auspices of its most illustrious founder, by institutions which have been able to reconcile Union with liberty. This Union has been fruitful. It has exhibited to the world the spectacle of a prosperity without example in the annals of history ... this Union is not simply in our eyes an element essential to the universal *political* equilibrium—it constitutes, besides, a nation to which our August Master and all Russia have pledged the most friendly interests—for the two countries, placed at the extremities of the two worlds, both in the ascending period of their development, appear called to a natural community of interests and sympathies. . . .

DIPLOMATIC CORRESPONDENCE, 1862

THE LEVEL OF
HUMAN VALUES HAS FALLEN

The following extracts are from the diary of Prince Napoleon, son of Jerome Bonaparte and cousin of Napoleon III. In the summer of 1861 the

Prince, sometimes known as "Plon Plon," arrived in America with his wife and a party of friends which included Lieutenant-Colonel Ferri Pisani and Maurice Sand, whose reports of the visit appear elsewhere in this book.

A visit to President Lincoln at noon, at the White House. . . . Mr. Seward, the Secretary of State, was the first to arrive. There was not a servant in sight, not even a doorman. You just walked in, as you would into a café. Mr. Seward is a little old man, who looks very much like a schoolteacher; very intelligent, very shrewd, rather bad-mannered, self-important and conceited, who talks with great fluency and affability. He is said to be the political brain of the government and is entirely responsible for the President's foreign policy. He looked frankly dingy, was wearing a coat of undefined color, a piece of string for a necktie, and a large straw hat.

A few minutes later, Mr. Lincoln entered the room. He is a very tall, lean man, who looks rather like a bootmaker and seemed embarrassed. He wore a closely clipped beard with no mustache, was dressed in a black suit. After shaking hands with me, we both sat down. He hardly said a word, and then nothing but commonplaces. I gathered, however, that he was asking Mr. Seward whether my father was named Lucien or Jerome. After some ten minutes of that kind of thing I became bored and took my leave. What a difference between this sad representative of the great republic and its early founders! This is a compromise President who was elected simply because people could not agree on some more prominent figure. I fear that the level of human values has fallen considerably. Mr. Lincoln is a worthy enough man, a lawyer from Illinois, and a one-time carpenter, unless I am mistaken. But he's a poor specimen of a President, and they tell me here that he is the commonest they have had thus far. . . .

The French visitors call on the Confederate leaders:

When we reached General Johnston's headquarters around seven o'clock, General Beauregard had just arrived. He is a Louisiana creole who speaks perfect French, a Catholic and a West Pointer. Vain, loquacious, extraordinarily sure of himself, he talks like a victorious leader. Johnston is more modest, more reserved, and what he says is always well-founded.

We were given a warm reception by the officers, Colonel Prescott and Colonel Lee, and the Southern planters gathered there for the occasion. The conversation turned to Bull Run, which had excited and elated them considerably. They're quite sure of winning the war and insist that they want separation from the North at all costs, since they consider the Union no longer exists. Northerners, for them, are foreigners; they have amended the Constitution, they have their own government in Richmond, and declare themselves to be an agricultural nation that sells its produce to England and France. Slavery is never mentioned, but it is implied when they say that they are the "guardians of their fathers' institutions."

It is quite remarkable that both here and in the

North people quite pointedly avoid all mention of the only true, real cause of this war, which is slavery, of course. The South's ideas are not sound and what they say makes no sense. I doubt too if any of their statesmen really believes in the possibility of their being able to exist as a separate nation based on slavery. But all compromise has now become impossible. As far as the South is concerned, the only acceptable bases for negotiation are independence and withdrawal from the Union. For any sort of arrangement to be possible, therefore, the North will have to win an important victory. Public opinion in the North, although extremely worked up would, I believe, make great sacrifices to maintain the Union. The actual crisis is a grave one. But I have every confidence in the good common sense and the tenacity of the American people.

Prince Napoleon, VOYAGE AUX ETATS-UNIS ET AU CANADA

"I FEEL FOR MY FRIENDS
BOTH NORTH AND SOUTH"

Swedish novelist Fredrika Bremer was a prolific writer and a champion of social reform. She came to the United States in 1849 and traveled extensively in this country for the next two years. Her literary and social contacts here were tremendous, among them being such literary giants of mid-nineteenth-century America as Emerson, Hawthorne, Irving, Longfellow and Lowell. Women leaders in the reform movement, including Dorothea Dix, Julia Ward Howe and Lucretia Mott were just a few of the Americans who became good friends and admirers of this extraordinary woman. When the war started, Fredrika Bremer's sympathies were deeply involved, for she had good friends on both sides. However, she favored the North, as shown by the following letter written in August of 1861 to Justina Howland, a Southerner, and in subsequent letters to her New York friends, Mr. and Mrs. Marcus Spring, which appear later in this book.

Out of the peace of my country and home I send many an anxious glance over the ocean to the great new world which I have felt as the home of generous hearts, and now alas, the scene of civil war! God be praised that you and your family are no more in the South, where to live now would be next to death to such minds as yours, and where every day must be full of fear and terror as I think of it. God be thanked that you are in the free north linked to it in welfare as you always were in sympathies. I feel no doubt as to the issue of this war, but much blood and much bitterness may come of it ere it results in peace. I feel for my friends both north and south, feel for the generous hearts in both parts of the disunited union, and for the putting off of the good works of peace. But works of charity and moral fortitude will take their place; public and private calamity will work more seriousness, a higher tone of life, and, I have no doubt, a better state of society. Much do I hope for a nobler turn in the aspirations of American women throughout the land.

Signe A. Rooth, SEERESS OF THE NORTHLAND

A CREATION OF HUMAN REASON

Eugène Forcade was known throughout Europe for his "Chronique de la Quinzaine," a bimonthly column which appeared in the *Revue des Deux Mondes.* He was a brilliant writer and economist, whose penetrating, well-informed analyses of the European and American political and economic scene revealed a man of strong liberal convictions. Through his columns, Forcade played an important role in explaining to the French public the issues at stake in the Civil War. The following are excerpts from his widely read column.

August 15, 1861— . . .France, as well, would appear to be wounded in a most vital spot by this blow that has severed the Union. . . . For more than any other government in this modern world of ours the American government possessed the distinctive characteristic of being a creation of human reason. Under its profoundly rational Constitution, full equality co-existed and was consistent with the most complete liberty. It represented the ideal of social and political justice which every human society seeks to attain. And even to men of intellect, living in countries where they cannot look forward to social and political justice in the immediate future, even to these men, the government of the United States offered consolation. For it allowed them to point with pride to a brilliant example of a rational conception of statecraft.

We feel somehow humbled and certainly very distressed by this deplorable Civil War into which the United States are now plunged, simply because it may very well bring about the failure of a society built upon human reason. Nor can we understand that such a spectacle should not have fired the better minds of France and of all Europe with heroic resolution. Why would it not be possible for distinguished Frenchmen, Englishmen, Italians and Germans to offer their mediation to the divided Americans? We would not advise the governments of these countries to venture upon such an undertaking for it might easily appear to have been prompted by selfish motives and considered as an intolerable piece of interference. But private individuals, eminent men, liberal-minded men well known throughout the world might be persuaded to act as mediators. The volunteers who fought with Washington had not been commissioned to do so by the Court of Versailles. On the contrary, they acted against the will of their government, and compelled, by their action, this same gov-

ernment to follow suit. Could not present-day Europe
do the same?

September 15, 1861—How is it possible to wage war
on such a scale without a permanent army? And is
the existence of a standing army compatible with
American institutions? And would not a powerful
military organization give rise to a whole lot of new
customs, new ambitions, new motives as regards both
private and public careers? . . . The men responsible
for the fate of the American union must certainly be
aware of these dangers. Everything cries out to them:
"This war must be a short one!" But the regiments
are completely lacking in discipline and desertion is
frequent. They have no confidence in their generals,
their army lost its first battle and the enemy has now
gained the offensive. All of this explains why the
American government has gone so far as to threaten
the South with the horrors of a war in which the
Negroes would have been called upon to take up
arms. It also explains why the American government
has been forced to ask Europe to send them a general.
This general is Garibaldi—and he has accepted the
post offered him. The mystic hero of all the wars of
independence fought in our epoch has probably been
persuaded to accept because of the humanitarian nature of this war. The great cause of the abolition of
slavery was what determined his gesture and this fact
constitutes for us a guarantee that the North will
from now on openly wage war for the emancipation
of the slaves.

Eugène Forcade, REVUE DES DEUX MONDES

GENERAL FRÉMONT ACTS
AS PROCONSUL

Lieutenant-Colonel Camille Ferri Pisani, aide-de-camp to the Prince, accompanied the Prince and his party on their visit to America in 1861. An intelligent and keen observer, he kept a journal of the trip in the form of letters to a colleague in Paris. Because he was a member of such a distinguished entourage, Ferri Pisani had ample opportunity to come into direct contact with the political and military leaders of both sides of the conflict. The following are excerpts from a recent translation of Colonel Ferri Pisani's book which was first issued in Paris in 1862.

St. Louis, September 5, 1861

Just as the government—on the brink of the abyss —called on McClellan to defend the Potomac, Frémont was sent to the Mississippi. Soon after his arrival, Frémont acted as a proconsul; by enforcing martial law he concentrated power in his hands: He raises troops, forms army corps, appoints or confirms officers, and worries little, I believe, about Washington. Requisitions in money make provision for army funds and nature takes care of the soldiers' needs. He has arrogated to himself the right to expel or arrest citizens, to suppress newspapers—although he does not seem to exercise these powers to the limit—thus frightening the population. More than 40,000 people have left St. Louis.

Such is the situation of one of the most important states of the American Republic. Similar conditions are often found in Europe, but in the United States, this is so extraordinary and rare that no other traveler can claim to have witnessed such a spectacle.

Today, September 5, Prince Napoleon devoted part of the morning to General Frémont's visit. Then he visited him at his camp and met his principal lieutenants. . . .

General Frémont was the unruly child of the Republican party, or rather he had the nerve and audacity to compromise and embarrass those colleagues whom he does not like while ensuring his own political future. Convinced that sooner or later the abolitionist idea must triumph in the Union and that the possibility of compromise with the South is nothing but a dream—a dream that the present war must have dissipated—he moved ahead. By expressing what clever ones have thus far not dared to admit, by taking the lead in a movement which will soon carry everyone with it, he gained for himself a position higher than that of all the men he had outrun. A few days before our arrival in St. Louis, he issued a proclamation ordering, within the whole area under his command, the confiscation of property and immediate freedom of all slaves belonging to citizens who

84

declared themselves against the Union. You notice the very important shade of meaning. What is serious, is not the confiscation of people's properties, although for us administrative and military confiscation is a monstrosity; the capital point is the distinction established in the General's decree between the property represented by a slave, and the property represented by a house or a plantation. That the slave be confiscated is so much the better! Thus he can be sold for the benefit of the Public Treasury, just as the house and the plantation will be auctioneered! But to free him is an innovation the importance of which escapes no one. This is to recognize that the abolition of slavery is the principal aim of the war, and to create between North and South an abyss that even piles of corpses will not suffice to fill.

General Frémont's proclamation burst over Washington like thunder. The sensation was immense, as is the case whenever an audacious mouth dares to shout the words which others dare only to whisper, or whenever a bright light suddenly lightens the half-darkness of a situation obscured by lies. Every day New York newspapers declare that General Frémont is disavowed, and that he has been called to Washington to account for his conduct. So far, no such thing has been done! The Cabinet, in Washington, is quite embarrassed; they play dead and pretend not to have heard of his proclamation. But everyone knows how perplexed the Cabinet is. . . .

We had been more or less told that the Army of the West was almost entirely composed of recently arrived emigrants, especially Germans. I must confess that I did not expect such a strong foreign character. It practically isolates the army from the rest of the population. This army was mainly recruited in the

Western states where the German element is predominant, and in the state of Missouri. Since in Missouri the French and English population generally favor the South, recruiting was limited to the very numerous German settlers and all partisans of the North. We were told that in St. Louis alone there were 30,000 inhabitants who, though American citizens, were born in Germany.

The predominance of the German element in the Army of the West is therefore the result of the nature of the sources which fed the recruitment of volunteers. Many causes forced the Germans to serve the flag. First, the high pay of soldiers, an almost irresistible attraction for wretched emigrants who left their country because of their misfortune, and who, if they found bread in their new motherland, were nonetheless forced to earn it daily with their sweat. Moreover, Germany is the traditional land of professional soldiers. Germans embrace the military profession willingly, and not so long ago, they served as mercenaries in many of the world's armies. These tastes and traditions follow the men of Hesse, Württemberg, and Prussia, wherever they go, and disappear only after several generations.

Finally, must I say it? Most Germans who come to America nowadays bring along a kind of hatred for the political regime of their fatherland, a democratic sentiment less pure from traces of envy than that of the older Americans. They have sometimes a background of latent socialism; in the United States this feeling would be considered as madness, but nevertheless it is working at the bottom of their souls. In Missouri, the man who represents best, in German eyes, aristocracy and fortune—the objects of his dislike—is the slaveowner. This explains the instinct which leads these people, as a whole, to enlist under the flag of abolitionism, and now under the flag of the Union. The German element played an important role in the electoral success of Mr. Lincoln, and now is at the basis of the extreme popularity and the political future of General Frémont.

His arrival in St. Louis gave a livelier impulse to the spirit which presided in the Army of the West at the beginning of the war. The predominance of the German element has now been turned into the systematic exclusion of all others. The numerous staff of General Frémont only includes one American. His chief of staff is Colonel Asboth, an Hungarian officer; he was Kossuth's friend [Hungarian patriot and statesman] and came to America with him. The chief of the engineer corps is a Bavarian. Several aides-de-camp come from the Rhineland, Germans mixed with a little French. The two officers who have been dispatched to serve the Prince are a German-speaking Swiss, Colonel Joliat, and a former Prussian lieutenant, Colonel Osterhaus. . . .

Still, on the whole, I am convinced that there are excellent military qualities in all those German officers. Without them and without the energetic appeal of the German population, the whole of Missouri would have been lost to the Union after the defeat of Springfield. The leader of the German military party is General [Franz] Sigel, a former officer in the Baden army. When part of this army revolted in 1848, he sided with the insurrection, and Sigel was forced to emigrate to America. Thirteen years later, his military talents found an employment which he had certainly not foreseen. When the army of the volunteers of the West was created, Sigel was elected general because of his experiences in 1848 and because of his

87

influence over the German emigrants—many of whom are more or less "volunteer" political exiles. Later his election was implemented by an appointment. . . .

If one were to meet this striking personality in Germany, one would undoubtedly say: "There is the very type of German revolutionary and socialist." But in this fortunate American country, one must admit, there are neither socialists nor revolutionaries. When one of these terrifying doctrines, which shake and ruin our older societies, reaches this country, it is absorbed; it melts, evaporates, and disappears in contact with individualism.

Ferri Pisani, PRINCE NAPOLEON IN AMERICA, 1861

CONTRASTING POINTS OF VIEW

William Howard Russell, commenting in his *My Diary North and South* on foreign volunteers in the Union forces, had this to say:

It is strange that this great, free and civilized Union should be supported by Germans . . . who plunder and destroy as if they were living in the days of Agricola.

Whereas August Laugel, French political writer, observed in his *Les Etats-Unis Pendant la Guerre:*

It was among the Germans that one could find the most exalted defenders of the Union, the most resolute enemies of slavery. Having grasped from the beginning the character and the object of the civil war, they have espoused the cause of the Union and of emancipation with an ardor and a passion, the influence of which has been felt even in Europe by the population beyond the Rhine.

"I WOULD WALK BAREFOOT
TO THE END OF THE EARTH"

Richard Cobden has made a place for himself in English history as a liberal statesman, parliamentarian and political writer. Although a wealthy industrialist, he devoted all of his efforts to advance liberal and humanitarian causes. With his friend, John Bright, Cobden played a major role in arousing public opinion in England to favor the North. The following letter is addressed to the Reverend Henry Richard, Cobden's colleague and editorial writer on the *Morning and Evening Star,* a paper owned by Cobden.

Dear Richard:

I hope there is no truth in the rumour that our Government will acknowledge the Southern confederacy. I have great faith in their stupidity and ignorance, and still more in their false and selfish predilections in all cases where liberty and the true interests of the millions are concerned, but can hardly believe them bad enough for this.

J. A. Hobson, RICHARD COBDEN, THE INTERNATIONAL MAN

Cobden gloomily predicts Europe's attitude toward secession in a letter to his friend Mr. Paulton.

December, 1861

I can't see my way through the American business. I don't believe the North and South can ever lie in the same bed again. Nor can I see how the military operations can be carried into the South, so as to inflict a crushing defeat. Unless something of the kind takes place I predict that Europe will recognize the independence of the South. I will tell Sumner this, and tell him that his only chance if he wants time to fight it out is to raise the blockade of the Mississippi voluntarily, and then Europe might look on.

But our friend Bright will not hear anything against the claims of the North. I admire his pluck, for when he goes with a side it is always to win. I tell him that it is possible to wish well to a cause without being sure that it will be successful. However, he will soon find in the House that we shall be on this question, as we were on China, Crimean and Greek-Pacifico wars, quite in a minority. There is no harm in that if you are right, but it is useless to deceive ourselves about the issue. *Three-fourths of the House will be glad to find an excuse for voting for the dismemberment of the Great Republic.*

John Bigelow, RETROSPECTIONS OF AN ACTIVE LIFE

Toward the end of 1862 Cobden still continues in a pessimistic vein to the Reverend Henry Richard.

October 15, 1862

Dear Richard:

I made up my mind during the Crimean war that if ever I lived in the time of another great war of a similar kind between England and another power, I would not as a public man open my mouth on the subject, so convinced am I that appeals to reason, conscience or interest have no force whatever on parties engaged in war, and that exhaustion of one or both sides can alone bring a contest of physical force to an end. Such being my view with regard to a war in which our own country is engaged, it is still more strongly applicable to the case of a foreign country. Unless compelled incidentally to allude to it, I shall not say a syllable in public upon the subject of this horrible American war. I need hardly add that I would walk barefoot to the end of the earth if, by so doing, I could put an end to the sanguinary struggle.

J. A. Hobson, RICHARD COBDEN, THE INTERNATIONAL MAN

HAPPY RESULTS TO THE SAFETY OF EUROPE

Although he achieved only a minor reputation in this country for his historical novels, Sir Edward Bulwer-Lytton was a prolific and popular novelist and playwright in mid-nineteenth-century England. In addition he pursued an active political career as a member of Parliament and was appointed Colonial Secretary in 1858. An extreme conservative, Bulwer-Lytton was uncompromisingly pro-South in his speeches and writings. The following is an excerpt from a speech before the Herts Agricultural Society, September 25, 1861.

I never conceived, nor do I understand how any far-thinking statesman could conceive, that a fourth part of the earth could long be held under one imperial form of government. That separation between North and South America which is now being brought about by civil war I have long foreseen and foretold to be inevitable, and I venture to predict that the younger men here present will live to see not two, but at least four . . . separate and sovereign commonwealths arising out of those populations which a year ago united their Legislature under one President and carried their merchandise under a single flag. And so far from thinking that these separations will be injurious to the future destinies of America . . . I believe that such separations will be attended with happy results to the safety of Europe and the development of American civilization. If it could have been possible that, as population and wealth increased, all the vast continent of America, with her mighty seaboard and the fleets which her increasing ambition as well as her extending commerce would have formed and armed, could have remained under one form of government . . . why, then, America would have hung over Europe like a gathering and destructive thunder-cloud. No single kingdom in Europe could have been strong enough to maintain itself against a nation that had once consolidated the gigantic resources of a quarter of the globe. . . .

But in proportion as America shall become subdivided into different States, each of which is . . . larger than an European kingdom—her ambition will be less formidable to the rest of the world. . . . I am not, then, one of those who say that the impending separation of the American States proves the failure of her experiment of democracy. . . . But this I may say . . . when we see an American President so bewildered by his own armies, or so despairing of the skill of his own generals, that he offers to the Italian Garibaldi the command of American patriots—I think, without vanity . . . that America has more to learn from England than England can learn from America.

John Bigelow, RETROSPECTIONS OF AN ACTIVE LIFE

MEN AND ANGELS MUST WEEP

Anthony Trollope, the author of the successful Barsetshire series, was the son of the Frances Trollope who had written so harshly about America in 1832 in her *Domestic Manners of the Americans.* Trollope was a minor official in the British postal service when he secured a leave of nine months for the express purpose of visiting the America his mother had so ridiculed and reviled thirty years before. He arrived with his wife in September, 1861, and returned to England in March, 1862, their visit coinciding with the height of the Trent Affair. Trollope published his impressions of the trip in a volume called *North America,* from which an excerpt follows.

Of all countries in the world one would say that the States of America should have been the last to curse themselves with a war; but now the curse has fallen upon them with a double vengeance. It would seem that they could never be great in war: their very institutions forbid it; their enormous distances forbid it; the price of labour forbids it; and it is forbidden also by the career of industry and expansion which has been given to them. But the curse of fighting has come upon them, and they are showing themselves to be as eager in the works of war as they have shown themselves capable in the works of peace. Men and angels must weep as they behold the things that are being done, as they watch the ruin that has come and is still coming, as they look on commerce killed and agriculture suspended. No sight so sad has come upon the earth in our days. They were a great people; feeding the world, adding daily to the mechanical appliances of mankind, increasing in population beyond all measures of such increase hitherto known, and extending education as fast as they extend their numbers. Poverty had as yet found no place among them, and hunger was an evil of which they had read, but were themselves ignorant. Each man among their crowds had a right to be proud of his manhood. To read and write,—I am speaking here of the North,— was as common as to eat and drink. To work was no disgrace, and the wages of work were plentiful! To live without work was the lot of none. What blessing above these blessings was needed to make a people great and happy? And now a stranger visiting them would declare that they are wallowing in a very slough of despond. The only trade open is the trade of war. The axe of the woodsman is at rest; the plough is idle; the artificer has closed his shop. The roar of the foundry is still heard because cannon are needed, and the river of molten iron comes out as an implement of death. The gold of the country is hiding itself as though it had returned to its mother-earth, and the infancy of a paper currency has been commenced.

These people speak our language, use our prayers, read our books, are ruled by our laws, dress themselves in our image, are warm with our blood. They have all our virtues; and their vices are our own too, loudly as we call out against them. They are our sons and our daughters, the source of our greatest pride, and as we grow old they should be the staff of our age. Such a war as we should now wage with the States would be an unloosing of hell upon all that is best upon the world's surface.

Anthony Trollope, NORTH AMERICA

NOTES FROM THE BELGIAN PRESS

October 2, 1861—To what is due the slowing down of our exports? Plain good sense shows that the commercial treaties have nothing to do with it since they have opened important markets for our products which were closed for us. The truth is that the Civil War which is ravishing North America is the sole cause of this period of non-activity.

Not only has it totally suspended our commerce with the former United States, but in striking an even more violent blow at the commercial prosperity of

England it has also restricted as a quite natural consequence the consumption faculties of that country.

MONITEUR BELGE

December 22, 1861—Among the documents which were exchanged with the representative of the United States at Berlin, we find one dated May 8th stating that M. de Schlenitz, Foreign Affairs Minister of Prussia has given assurance of the most positive kind that his government, in principle consistently opposed to revolutionary movements, would be one of the last to recognize any governments de facto of the Secessionist States of the American Union . . .

MONITEUR BELGE

LETTERS FROM KING LEOPOLD
TO QUEEN VICTORIA

Leopold, King of the Belgians, writes to his niece Queen Victoria expressing his views on the situation in America. The "Paris" and "Robert" he refers to in the letter immediately following are the comte de Paris and the duc de Chartres. Both young men came to this country with their uncle, the

Prince de Joinville, and with him joined McClellan's Army of the Potomac. In the second letter Leopold states his solution to the American problem briefly and succinctly.

Laeken, 17th October 1861

My Beloved Victoria:

... I regret much Paris and Robert having joined the Federal Army, mixing in a civil war!! The object is to show courage, to be able to say: *"Ils se sont beaucoup distingués."* They have a chance of being shot for Abraham Lincoln and the most rank Radicalism. I don't think that step will please in France, where Radicalism is at discount fortunately. The poor Queen is very unhappy about it, but now nothing can be done, only one may wish to see them well out of it. Poor Queen! ...

Your devoted and only Uncle,
Leopold R.

A. C. Benson and Viscount Esher, eds.,
LETTERS OF QUEEN VICTORIA

Laeken, 20th November 1862

My Beloved Victoria:

... The point of most vital importance to England is, that there should be two great Republics, instead

of one, the more so as the South can never be manufacturing, and the North, on the contrary, is so already to a great extent, and actually in so many markets a rival. . . .

George Earle Buckle, ed., LETTERS OF QUEEN VICTORIA

"WE HAVE NO TROUBLES BUT PUBLIC TROUBLES"

George Eliot comments on the war in
letters to friends:

October 23, 1861

To Mrs. Congreve:

I am in the happiest and most contented mood and
have only good news to tell you. I have hardly any
trouble nearer to me than the American war and the
prospects of the poor cotton weavers. . . .

February 15, 1862

To Madame Bodichon:

We have had no troubles but public troubles—
anxiety about the War with America. . . . My best
consolation is that an example on so tremendous a

99

scale [as the war] of the need of education of mankind through the affections and sentiments, as a basis for true development, will have a strong influence on all thinkers, and be a check to the arid narrow antagonism which in some quarters is held to be the only liberal form of thought. . . .

J. W. Cross, ed., GEORGE ELIOT'S LIFE AS RELATED IN HER LETTERS

THE TRENT AFFAIR

The *Trent* was a British mail steamer returning to Europe from Cuba. On November 8, 1861, it was stopped at sea by the *San Jacinto,* a Northern naval vessel whose captain, Charles Wilkes, ordered a shot fired across the *Trent's* bow. Captain Wilkes then proceeded to remove John Slidell, the Southern envoy to the French court, and John Mason, the Confederacy's designated minister to London. England and France, but especially England, howled and raged. It was incorrectly assumed in both those countries that Wilkes had acted on orders from Washington and thus it appeared that the United States had violated the rights of a neutral ship.

The incident brought England and the United States almost to the brink of war. In the heat of the furor raised in England, the London *Morning Chronicle* wrote on November 28, 1861:

Abraham Lincoln, whose accession to power was generally welcomed on this side of the Atlantic, has proved himself a feeble, confused, and little-minded mediocrity; Mr. Seward, the firebrand at his elbow, is exerting himself to provoke a quarrel with all Europe, in that spirit of senseless egotism which induces the Americans, with their dwarf fleet and shapeless mass of incoherent squads, which they call an army, to fancy themselves the equals of France by land and of Great Britain by sea. If the Federal States could be rid of these two mischief-makers, it might yet redeem itself in the sight of the world; but while they stagger on at the head of affairs, their only chance of fame consists in the probability that the navies of England will blow out of the water their blockading squadrons, and teach them how to respect the flag of a mightier supremacy beyond the Atlantic.

A more detailed introduction to John Bright, the leading supporter of the North in Parliament, will appear later in this book. At this point, however, an excerpt from his speech at Rochdale, December 4, 1861, follows.

There has occurred an event which has been announced to us only a week ago which is one of great importance, and it may be one of some peril. It is asserted that what is called international law has been broken by a steamer of war of the United States. The act which has been committed by the American steamer, in my opinion, whether it is legal or not, is both impolitic and bad. I think it will turn out, and is almost certain, that so far as the taking of these men from that ship was concerned, it was wholly unknown to and unauthorized by the American Government; and that if the American Government believes, on the opinion of its officers, that the act is illegal, I have no doubt that they will make fitting reparation. Our great adviser, the *Times* newspaper, has been persuading the people that this is but one of a series of acts which denote the determination of the Washington government to pick a quarrel with the people of England. Do you believe that the United States Government, presided over by President Lincoln, so constitutional in all his acts, so moderate as he has been—do you believe that that government, having upon its hands now an insurrection of the most formidable character in the South, would invite the armies and the fleets of England to combine with that insurrection, and it might be so to exasperate the struggle as to render it impossible that the Union should ever again be restored?

What can be now more monstrous than that we, who call ourselves to some extent an educated, a moral, and Christian nation, the moment that any accident of this kind occurs, before we have made a representation to the American Government, before we have had a word from them in reply, are all up in arms, every sword is leaping from its scabbard,

and every man is looking out for his pistols and his
blunderbuss.

John Bright, "A FRIENDLY VOICE FROM ENGLAND
ON AMERICAN AFFAIRS"

As British opinion was being whipped
to a frenzy for war by Tories in and
out of Parliament and the ultra-con-
servative press, led by the *Times,*
Bright was one of the few national
leaders who remained calm and reasonable in the crisis. In a series of
letters to Senator Charles Sumner, he
expressed his anxieties and hopes as
to the outcome of the Affair. The
following are excerpts from his letters
to Sumner.

Rochdale, December 14, 1861

There is less passion shown here than there was a
week ago, and there has been a considerable expression of opinion in favor of moderate counsels, and
urging arbitration rather than war. The unfavorable
symptom is the war preparations of the Government
and the sending of troops to Canada. . . . I know
nothing but what is in the papers; but I conclude that
this Government is ready for war if an excuse can be
found for it. . . . If you are resolved to succeed against
the South, *have no war with England;* make every
concession that can be made; don't even hesitate to
tell the world *that you will even concede what two*

years ago no Power would have asked of you, rather than give another nation a pretence for assisting in the breaking up of your country. . . .

Rochdale, December 21, 1861

The *Times* and other journals, but the *Times* chiefly, have sought to create the opinion that your Government, and Mr. Seward principally, seeks war with England. . . . Unfortunately whilst heretofore cotton has been the great bond of peace between the United States and England, *now* it is acting in a contrary direction. Men think whatever the evils of war with you, at least it would give us cotton—they care little for the monstrous cost, if the price is war—and thus cotton acts at this moment rather adversely than favorably to peace. . . . I believe opinion in Europe is against you on the *Trent* seizure, and that any concession you can make will obtain you much good will in Europe. . . .

When the stormy Affair blew over and war between England and America was averted, Bright wrote to Sumner:

Rochdale, January 11, 1862

I need not tell you how much I rejoice. . . . The warmongers here are baffled for the time, and I cannot but believe that a more healthy opinion is gradually extending itself on all matters connected with your great struggle. . . .

104

The London *Times,* however, was far
from rejoicing over the peaceful conclusion to an episode which it had
found ideal for provoking war between
the two countries. On January 11,
1862, it declared:

The ferocity and vindictiveness which have become
in the present generation part of the American character, as shown by duels and assassinations, and atrocities on board ship that almost pass belief, are now in
full play in this unhappy strife. And as yet the passions
of the combatants have hardly had scope. When the
half million of Northern soldiers are launched against
their adversaries, we may look for deeds such as the
warfare of hereditary rivals like England and France
would never know. . . .

PROCEEDINGS OF THE MASSACHUSETTS HISTORICAL SOCIETY

Le National, a Belgian newspaper,
summed up the Affair quite differ-
ently, on the same date, January 11,
1862:

Messers Mason and Slidell are now restored—restored with good grace. The crisis is passed and the
Times, whose blusterings had all contributed toward
envenoming the question, expresses its unreserved
satisfaction. Little does it matter to them that the
reparations were made unwillingly, with bitterness,
with threats even.

But the real differences at stake—don't they still

exist? Must we have illusions and imagine that the kidnapping of the Southern agents, the slur cast upon the flag of England—were the only things in question? Let us say rather that public opinion in Great Britain, led astray a moment by material interests and by other considerations perhaps less worthy, finds itself happy to have a pretext for regaining its true direction. Let the party of peace triumph then, but let it watch— let it be on guard against those dangerous surprises which may compromise a whole century of progress. What removes from President Lincoln's act any weakness of character or humility that may be attributed to him is the favorable situation of the United States army and the successes it is having.

"I SHALL FIND THIS HATING YOU VERY HARD WORK"

Letter from Charles Darwin to Asa Gray:

Down, December 11 [1861]

My dear Gray,—

Many and cordial thanks for your two last most valuable notes. What a thing it is that when you receive this we may be at war, and we two be bound, as good patriots, to hate each other, though I shall find this hating you very hard work. How curious it is to see two countries, just like two angry and silly men, taking so opposite a view of the same transaction. I fear there is no shadow of doubt we shall fight if the two Southern rogues are not given up. [Commissioners Slidell and Mason.] And what a wretched thing it will be if we fight on the side of slavery! No doubt it will be said we fight to get cotton; but I fully believe that this has not entered into the motive in the least. Well, thank Heaven, we private individuals have nothing to do with so awful a responsibility. Again, how curious it is that you seem to think that you can conquer the South; and I never meet a soul, even those who would most wish it, who thinks it possible—that is, to conquer and retain it. I do not suppose the mass of people in your country will believe it, but I feel sure if we do go to war it will be with the utmost reluctance by all classes, Ministers of Government and all. Time will show, and it is no use writing or thinking about it. . . .

Yours most cordially,
C. Darwin.

Francis Darwin, LIFE AND LETTERS OF CHARLES DARWIN

"I CAN MAKE NO WAR IN MY SOUL"

Among the many artists and writers who made Italy their second homeland in the mid-1850's were the poet

Robert Browning and the American sculptor William Wetmore Story. A member of a distinguished Boston family, Story was a graduate of Harvard and when he was chosen to do a statue of his father, Supreme Court Justice Joseph Story, he went to Italy to study sculpture. His studio became a meeting place for the expatriate and European intellectual elite and it was during this period that a lifelong friendship first began between Browning and Story. Browning left Italy after his wife Elizabeth Barrett Browning died in 1861 and the following are excerpts from letters he wrote to Story after he settled in England.

November 10, 1861
1 Chichester Road
Upper Westburne Terrace

It is not because I do not feel the deepest interest in the American news that I rather turn from writing about it . . . particularly to you who understand so much more, foresee and perhaps apprehend more than can the uninstructed here. The grin of the ——— [*Times*] may be hard to bear, but indeed the feeling of the few people I see is altogether free from its malicious self-satisfaction. I never heard a word for the South, even from those who think the North underestimated its strength and despair of a better issue than separation. *We* say fight it out to the last, but for English lookers-on who abjure heroics to say

that, would be saying, "Do yourselves as much harm
as you can."

Dearest Friend—and dearer than ever just now!

. . . I think English judgment of the Northern pro-
cedures has been wrong from the beginning. . . .
Our people expected the pure and simple rights in
the case would be declared and vigourously carried
out without let or stop. "Slavery shall be abolished,
absolutely at once and forever." But at the first hesitation in the face of difficulties, we cried out, "Slavery
will not be extinguished after all," and our sympathy
stopped and our irritation began. . . . The *spirit* of
all Mr. Lincoln's acts is altogether against slavery in
the end, but in the apprehension of the result of los-
ing the uncertain states, he declared his intention
to be quite otherwise. *You* understand this and the
English did *not*. . . . Every measure now taken by the
North in the direction, plainer and plainer, of complete emancipation, will be considered as "forced
upon them," because our neutrality, poor, hard, cold
thing indeed, was the worst you had to expect and in
no moment of the fear of a terrible result for the
cotton operatives here, did any one dream of taking
part with the South. The sad affair of the "Trent"
puts all this away, however; our people hold to the
bone they have got in their jaws this time, that a
naval lieutenant is not an admiralty judge. . . .
Come what will, I, insignificant unit, can make no
war in my soul with my truest brother and friend. No

one ever had cause to love a country better than I, who have so long been only not an American, because people can hardly experience such generosity, except as strangers. Nor do I ever mean to go into the matter with you again, dearest of all American friends. . . .

December 31, 1861

. . . Indeed you are wrong as to men's "fury" here! I have not heard one man, woman or child express anything but dismay at the prospect of being obliged to go to war on any ground with America; but everyone felt there might be an obligation as stringent as a slap on the face from one's bosom friend. . . .

Henry James, WILLIAM WETMORE STORY AND HIS FRIENDS

MARX-ENGELS

CORRESPONDENCE CONTINUED

Engels to Marx:

November 27, 1861

Have these Yankees then gone completely crazy to carry out the mad coup with the Confederate Commissioners [Mason and Slidell]? The fact that here in the Channel too, a warship was waiting for the mail steamer, proves that general instructions must have been issued from Washington. To take political prisoners by force on a foreign ship, is the clearest *casus belli* there can be. The fellows must be sheer fools to land themselves in for a war with England. . . .

Marx to Engels:

December 9, 1861

War, as I have declared in the *Presse* from the first day, will not break out with America, and I only regret that I had not the means to exploit the asininity of the Reuter and *Times*-swayed Stock Exchange during this fool period.

Marx and Engels, THE CIVIL WAR IN THE UNITED STATES

IF ALL OTHER TONGUES
ARE SILENT

"We used to live for the transatlantic steamers that twice a week brought the anxiously expected news. America and its history, past and in the making, was the breath of our nostrils," explained one of John Bright's daughters when describing the intense family feeling during those tragic years of 1861–1865. John Bright, distinguished statesman and orator, was born the son of a Quaker cotton-mill owner in Lancashire. As a leading member of the then-emerging industrial middle class, Bright was a liberal politically and strongly anti-aristocratic. He and his parliamentary colleague, Richard Cobden, were probably the greatest English champions of the North and between them they were tremendously influential in turning English public opinion toward neutrality and, ultimately, in favor of the Union. Bright's passionate crusade was fought through speeches, in Parliament and out, in newspaper articles and in hundreds of letters addressed to policy makers involved in the American struggle.

From a speech at Rochdale, December 4, 1861:

In the crisis to which we have arrived now, I say that we, after all, are as much interested in the crisis of the North, as if I was making this speech in the city of Boston or New York. Twelve months ago, at the meeting of the Congress of the United States, there were various proposals made to try and devise some mode of settling the question between the North and South, so that the disunion might not go on; but though I read carefully everything that was published

I do not recollect that in any single instance the question of the tariff was referred to, or that any change was proposed or suggested in that matter as likely to have any effect upon the question of secession. If the tariff was onerous and grievous, was that a reason for this great insurrection? No; the question is a very different affair—a more grave question. It is the question of slavery. For thirty years it has been constantly coming to the surface, disturbing social life, and overthrowing almost all political harmony in the working of the United States. I think the man who says otherwise, and who contends that it is the tariff, or anything whatsoever other than slavery, is either himself deceived, or he endeavors to deceive others.

What is the course that England would be expected to pursue? We should be neutral so far as regards mingling in the strife. . . . Now, let us look a little at what has been said and done in this country since the period when Parliament rose in the beginning of August. There have been two speeches to which I wish to refer in terms of approbation. The Duke of Argyle delivered a speech which was fair and friendly to the Government of the United States. Lord Stanley made a speech which it is impossible to read without remarking the thought, the liberality, and the wisdom by which it was distinguished. I mention these two speeches as from noblemen of great distinction in this country—speeches which I believe would have a beneficial effect on the other side of the Atlantic. Lord John Russell, in the House of Commons, during the last session, made a speech, too, in which he rebuked the impertinence of a young member of the House of Commons who spoke about the bursting of the bubble republic—a speech worthy of the best days of Lord John Russell. . . . And if we part from the speakers and turn to the writers, what do we find there? We find that that journal which is reputed abroad, and has hitherto been reputed at home, as the most powerful representative of English opinion [the *Times*], at least of the richer classes—we find that in that very newspaper there has not been, since Mr. Lincoln took office, one fair, and honorable, and friendly article on American affairs in its columns. Some of you, I dare say, read it—but fortunately now every district is so admirably supplied with local newspapers, that I trust in all times to come the people of England will drink of purer streams nearer home. . . .

I want to know whether it has ever been admitted by politicians and statesmen that great nations can be broken up at any time by the will of any particular section of those nations? It has been said how much better it would be, not for the United States, but for us, if these states should be divided. I recollect meeting a gentleman in Bond Street before the session was over one day—a rich man, whose voice is very much heard on the opposite side to that on which I sit in the House of Commons—but whose voice is not heard when on his legs but when he is cheering other speakers. He said to me, "This is, after all, a sad business about the United States; but still I think it is much better that they should be split up. In twenty years (or fifty, I forget which it was he said) they will be so powerful that they will bully all Europe." And a distinguished member of the House of Commons, distinguished there for his eloquence, distinguished more by his many writings —I mean Sir Edward Bulwer-Lytton—he did not exactly express the hope, but he ventured on something like a prediction that the time would come when there would be as many republics and states in America as you can count upon your fingers. . . .

Our friends in America are in a great struggle.
There is nothing like it before in history. No country
in the world was ever more entitled, in my opinion, to
the sympathy and forbearance of all friendly countries than are the United States at this moment. There
is one thing which I must state where I think they
have a solid reason to complain. You recollect that,
during the session, on the 14th May, a proclamation
came out which acknowledged the South as a belligerent power, and proclaimed the neutrality of England.
A little time before that, I forget how many days,
Mr. Dallas, the last minister from the United States,
had left London for Liverpool and America. He
did not wish to undertake any affairs connected with
the government by which he had not been appointed,
the government of Mr. Lincoln, but to leave what
had to be done to his successor, who was on his way,
and whose arrival was daily expected. Mr. Adams, the
present minister from the United States, is a man, if
he lived in England, you would say was from one of
the noblest families of the country. I think that his
father and his grandfather were Presidents of the
United States. His grandfather was one of the great
men who achieved the independence of the United
States. There is no family in that country having more
claims upon what I should call the veneration and
affection of the people than the family of Mr. Adams.
Mr. Adams arrived in London on the night of the
13th of May. On the 14th that proclamation to which
I have alluded was issued. It was known he was coming; he was not consulted; it was not delayed for a
day, though nothing pressed, that he might be notified
about it. I have the very best reasons for knowing
that there is no single thing that has happened during
the course of these events that has created more sur-

prise, more irritation, and more distrust in the United States with respect to this country, than the fact that that proclamation did not wait even one single day till the minister from America could come here, and till it could have been done with his consent and concurrence, and in that friendly manner that would have avoided all the unpleasantness that has occurred. . . .

Two centuries ago multitudes of the people of this country found a refuge on the North American continent, escaping from the tyranny of the Stuarts and from the bigotry of Laud. Many noble spirits from our country endeavored to establish great experiments in favor of human freedom on that continent. Bancroft, the greatest historian of his own country, has said, "The history of the colonization of America is the history of the crimes of Europe." From that time down to our own period America has admitted the wanderers from every clime. They subdued the wilderness. They met with plenty there, which was not afforded them in their native country, and they are become a great people. There may be those persons in England who are jealous of the States. There may be men who dislike democracy, and who hate a republic. There may even be those whose sympathies warm towards the slave oligarchy of the South. As for me, I have here this to say: If all other tongues are silent, mine shall speak for the policy which gives hope to the bondsmen of the South, and tends to generous thoughts, and generous words, and generous deeds between the two great nations who speak the English language, and from their origin are alike entitled to the English name.

John Bright,

"A FRIENDLY VOICE FROM ENGLAND ON AMERICAN AFFAIRS"

A TURNING POINT, FOR GOOD OR EVIL

John Stuart Mill, English philosopher and economist, came close to socialism in his advocacy of political and social reform. He was the author of many books and essays and his influence is felt even today in the field of economics, politics and philosophy. He was a strong supporter of the North and through letters, speeches and articles helped shift British opinion in favor of the North. The following excerpt is taken from his *Autobiography*.

The state of public affairs had become extremely critical, by the commencement of the American civil war. My strongest feelings were engaged in this struggle, which, I felt from the beginning, was destined to be a turning point, for good or evil, of the course of human affairs for an indefinite duration. Having been a deeply interested observer of the Slavery quarrel in America, during the many years that preceded the open breach, I knew that it was in all its stages an aggressive enterprise of the slave-owners to extend the territory of slavery; under the combined influences of pecuniary interest, domineering temper, and the fanaticism of a class for its class privileges. . . . Their success, if they succeeded, would be a victory of the powers of evil which would give courage to the enemies of progress and damp the spirits of its friends all over the civilized world, while it would create a formidable military power, grounded on the worst and most anti-social form of the tyranny of men over men, and, by destroying for a long time the prestige of the great democratic republic, would give to all the privileged classes of Europe a false confidence, probably only to be extinguished in blood. . . .

It may be imagined with what feelings I contemplated the rush of nearly the whole upper and middle classes of my own country, even those who passed for Liberals, into a furious pro-Southern partisanship: the working classes, and some of the literary and scientific men, being almost the sole exceptions of the general frenzy. I never felt so keenly how little permanent improvement had reached the minds of our influential classes, and of what small value were the liberal opinions they had got into the habit of professing. None of the Continental Liberals committed the same frightful mistake. . . .

England is paying the penalty, in many uncomfortable ways, of the durable resentment which her ruling classes stirred up in the United States by their ostentatious wishes for the ruin of America as a nation: they have reason to be thankful that a few, if only a few, known writers and speakers, standing firmly by the Americans in the time of their greatest difficulty, effected a partial diversion of these bitter feelings, and made Great Britain not altogether odious to the Americans.

AUTOBIOGRAPHY OF JOHN STUART MILL

PALMERSTON SENDS AN EARLY NEW YEAR GREETING TO THE QUEEN

At the time of the Civil War Viscount Palmerston was at the peak of his long and tumultuous career in the service of British diplomacy. Palmerston became Prime Minister in 1859 and, in the tradition of the great and domineering prime ministers, he frequently made decisions without consultation yet always succeeded in furthering British prestige. His attitude toward the war was avowedly neutral but his sympathies were clearly in favor of the South, particularly evidenced during the Trent Affair.

December 29, 1861

... This autumn and this winter, however, have been productive of events in three of the four quarters of the globe which future years are not likely to repeat. The capture of Pekin in Asia by British and French troops; the Union in Europe of nearly the whole of Italy under one monarchy; *and the approaching and virtually accomplished dissolution in America of the*

119

great Northern Confederation are events full of importance for the future as well as being remarkable in the present.

John Bigelow, RETROSPECTIONS OF AN ACTIVE LIFE

ENLISTMENTS AND EMIGRATION

During the decade 1850–1860 more than 2,600,000 Europeans came to the United States and a majority of them settled in the North. They came for a variety of reasons—a huge German migration after the events of 1848, the Irish after the potato famine, and all who came spread across the land in peaceful pursuit of whatever their goals. The Homestead Act of 1862 served as an impetus and irresistible lure, and American and European shipping and emigration officers in Europe facilitated the mass departures. With the outbreak of war, these officials doubled as enlistment officers for the Union Army. In many instances they were besieged by young men, eager for the free transportation, the promise of a salary, food, clothing, and possibly land for the three-year term of enlistment. Even as late as January,

1865, one George Boulanger, later General and French Minister of War (1886), sought service in the Federal armies of the United States. Ulysse Ladet, editor of *Le Temps,* wrote American Ambassador Bigelow in his behalf. Bigelow later remarked: "What would have been the effect upon the world's history had I encouraged, as I did not, the aspirations of the captain—I believe he was then only a captain—had he been invited to draw his sword for the Union, is one of those secrets of Providence which it would be difficult to probe." Inevitably guarantees were made by the enlistment officers that could not always be fulfilled and eventually the European press lashed out at the procedure. Foreign consuls wrote to their ambassadors in Washington and their ministries at home protesting some of the alleged illegalities perpetrated upon their citizens. Following are examples of press and diplomatic reaction, covering the period 1861–1864.

From the Belfast Ulster Observer, *spring, 1862*

Were America engaged in a contest with a foreign invader there would be a glory in sustaining her, and no country would more wildly leap to her assistance than Ireland. But she cannot and should not expect our countrymen to be her mercenaries in the present fratricidal struggle. We therefore implore our young men not to be cajoled into a course fraught with danger and dishonor. . . . Thousands of Irishmen have . . . fully proved their fidelity to their adopted country; their allegiance to the cause of freedom; and if President Lincoln still stands in need of human hecatombs, he should look elsewhere than to the decimated homes of Ireland for the victims.

From the Bremen Deutsche Auswanderungs-Zeitung, *March, 1863:*

We are now once again the steadfast advocate of the belief that emigration is not only a good thing for our German Fatherland in a political as well as social aspect, but that it is to be regretted that many more of its children do not seek the West. Under the circumstances [widespread unemployment in France, England and Ireland] it is certainly better for the working man to go abroad and settle there, where, as for instance in the United States, a homestead farm is proffered him as a free gift, with very many guarantees of a future, free from care about subsistence. Nor should the existing Civil War deter men from emigration to the United States, for we have always said, and hold to it that the manufacturer and husbandman of East and West will not be directly affected by it, as not being in the slightest manner mixed up in it.

From the Prague, Austria, Die Morgen Post,
March, 1863:

> Seward's circular No. 32 [the Homestead Act] is a
> common lie, a way to lure Austrian subjects to Amer-
> ica to enroll them in the army. . . .

Ella Lonn, FOREIGNERS IN THE UNION ARMY AND NAVY

Prussian Minister to Washington, Baron von
Grabow, to Secretary Seward, Septem-
ber 11, 1864:

> Numerous emigrants, who had just come from Ger-
> many to devote themselves to the ordinary agricul-
> tural and manufacturing occupations, have been
> turned from the objects of their voyage by being trans-
> ferred to an island in the port of Boston where, under
> the allurements of $100, promised in gold but paid
> in paper, they have been managed to be enlisted in
> the army. . . . Another vessel, having on board other
> emigrants, is momentarily expected in the bay of
> Boston, and everything leads to the belief that the
> same process will be followed in regard to them as
> to those who are already . . . at this time in the mili-
> tary service of the United States.

From the correspondence of Louis A.
Dochez, agent for emigration to the
United States in Brussels, to the editor
of L'Etoile Belge.

Sir: In your number of the 13th of October you re-
produced an article from the *Courier des Etats-Unis*
containing a letter dated at New York, September 20,
and signed by four emigrants, who complained bitterly of having been induced by my solicitations to
quit Belgium for the United States of America. These
emigrants say that I made them false promises; that
they emigrated expecting to engage in civil occupa-
tions there, and not to enlist as soldiers; that they
have been treated like dogs; and finally, that they
were turned loose in a foreign city, having been
presented with only one shirt and $7. . . .

There is, sir, one powerful reason which should
have made you suspicious of the veracity of the alle-
gations contained in the *Courier des Etats-Unis*. You
are well aware that this Bonapartist and pro-slavery
journal makes war to the knife against the government of the United States, and that the approach of
the presidential election has redoubled the violence
of the attacks of this partisan of the South against
the defenders of the Union. . . .

Since I returned from the United States in June,
1863, I have been engaged in two distinct enterprises
of emigration from Belgium.

The object of the first was to engage artisans for
civil labor in the United States, and especially miners
for the mines in the State of Illinois. In this enterprise
I acted as agent of various American corporations,
and, among others, of those who work the most important oil mines of the western States.

The second enterprise of emigration in which I
have co-operated commenced during the month of
July, 1864, and was completed on September 7. It had

for its purpose to facilitate the transportation of Belgians desirous to enlist in the military service of the United States.

In this connection, sir, I have to answer to the accusation of having deceived artisans by engaging them to emigrate to the United States for the purpose of subjecting them to military service there, while leading them to believe that they were emigrating to find there civil employment. That is an odious accusation. . . . To not one single emigrant who addressed himself to me since the establishment of my bureau . . . did I promise civil employment. Every single one who quitted Belgium emigrated with the intention of entering the military service of the United States, and with that intention and for that purpose solely. Every single one knew that he would not be able to obtain the promised bounty of $100, and receive the monthly pay of $12, and be clothed free of expense to himself for three years, except by enlisting as a soldier. . . . I further insert, in this connection, a copy of the circular which I addressed to most of the burgomasters of Belgium a little while after the opening of my bureau, and before the departure of the ships which transported the emigrants alluded to by the *Courier des Etats-Unis:*

Brussels, July 20, 1864

Sir: I have the honor to inform you that if in your town you have able-bodied unmarried men between the ages of twenty-one and forty years, who are poor and a public charge, you can, if you desire it, send them to engage in the service of the United States.

The following will be the conditions of such engagement:

1st. They enlist for three years' service.

2d. Their expenses of travel and of subsistence are paid from the places of their residence in Europe until the expiration of the three years.

3d. They receive a bounty of a hundred dollars upon their arrival in the United States.

4th. They are entitled to monthly pay of $12 during their three years' service, and are furnished, free of cost to themselves, during the entire term of their enlistment, with all their clothing and other military equipments.

It is absolutely necessary that, before the sixth of August next, you shall transmit to me a certificate of military service or of identity of such emigrants. That is needful to enable me to forward to you funds to pay the expenses of their travel in Europe to the port of embarkation.

You perceive, sir, that this circular could not leave any doubt as to the destination of these emigrants. It was to such as should desire to serve in the federal army that this appeal was addressed. To those alone were expectations held out of the bounty of $100, a pay of $12 per month, and all their clothing and military equipments. . . .

The enterprise, sir, in which the persons of whom I was the agent were engaged, was simply an enterprise of transportation; and it derived a legitimate remuneration of its expenses by assignment of a portion of the bounty paid by the United States to recruits. Neither the government of Belgium, nor that of the United States, had any concern whatsoever with it.

Although this enterprise was wholly unofficial in its character, there is no feature of it which any one concerned in it has any reason to conceal from public investigation and criticism. If we had reason to expect personal profit from it, it was of profit equally to the emigrants, to Belgium, and to the United States. The cause in behalf of which I have aided these Belgians to enlist is the cause of the Union against rebels who seek to destroy it. You may have of this cause whatever opinion you please. For myself, I consider it the cause of order and of civilization. . . .

On March 2, 1864, L. de Geofroy, French Chargé d'Affaires in Washington, addressed the following note to Secretary Seward:

Washington, March 2, 1864

Sir: A Frenchman, Mr. Cauvet, has addressed the department for foreign affairs at Paris, for the purpose of obtaining the liberation of his son, arbitrarily incorporated, as it would seem, in the federal army. M. Drouyn de Lhuys, in transmitting to me the extract annexed, from a letter, in which Mr. Cauvet, the son, states to his family the circumstances under which he was constrained to do military service, charges me to point out the fact to your excellency, when asking you to have the goodness to give such orders that Mr. Cauvet be stricken from the rolls and set free. . . .

Extract of letter from A. Couvet, the forcibly detained Frenchman, to Drouyn de Lhuys, Foreign Minister of France:

127

I am going to tell you something that will not give you much pleasure. I would tell you that I had hardly received your letter, when I settled my account at the house where I was, and came back to New York, where I staid some days, awaiting a vessel on which to return to France, but meanwhile persons came looking for me, and telling me I was a soldier, and that I must go, because my name had been given at the hotel where I was staying without my knowing anything about it, and told me that the chance had fallen on me. There were two of us in this situation, and we were told we could not be obliged to become soldiers, but we had no person to take care of us, and meantime we were taken to an island in the neighborhood, and gradually, a month afterwards, we were off to the city of Charleston, thoroughly enrolled in the regiment, and at the end of some days were carrying on our backs the knapsack and musket. . . .

DIPLOMATIC CORRESPONDENCE, 1864-1865

Diplomatic pressure for his release was either lost or ignored by the War Department and the young man was killed in the action at Drewry's Bluff, May 18, 1864.

"OUR GOVERNMENT IS MADE UP OF MEN DRAWN FROM THE ARISTOCRATIC FAMILIES"

Letter from John Bright to John Bigelow:

Rochdale, Jany. 3, 1862

... It is a great mistake to imagine that our people are against your people. Our Govt. is made up of men drawn from the aristocratic families—it is therefore aristocratic, and from a natural instinct, it must be hostile to your greatness & to the permanence of your institutions. Our rich men take their course mainly from the Aristocracy to whom they look up—and our Press, in London especially, is directly influenced by the Govt., and the two sections of the Aristocracy for which it writes—we have also our tremendous military services, with all their influence on the Govt. & on opinion. But we have other and better influences—the town populations—the nonconformist congregations, the quiet & religious people, and generally I believe the working men—these have done much to put down the war cry, and to make a very considerable demonstration in favor of moderation, & if needful of arbitration. . . .

I need hardly tell you that Mr. Cobden and I have done all we could by writing our intimate friends in this Govt. to urge them to moderation and peace. The Prime Minister is old, and steeped in the traditions of a past generation; he has made his only reputation by the pretence that he is plucky and instant in the defence of English honor, and he is in that condition just now that a revival of popularity is very needful for him. If foreign affairs are tranquil, his Govt. must break up. Bluster and occasionally war even have been resorted to by ministers in past times to sustain a tottering Statesman or a falling party, and I am not sure that some of our present ministers have a morality superior to that of their predecessors.

Let us hope, however, for good and for peace. I have great trust in the calmness and moderation of your President, and in the solid wisdom of your Senate. They must baffle our war-mongers, and show that it is not passion and anger that move them, and then give to the world an evidence of their capacity to steer their great ship, with its freight of freedom and blessings for the whole human race, through the stormiest seas.

Your letter is very kind, and gave much pleasure—I value your good opinion highly—I am glad too to know that Mrs. Bigelow thinks I have done some justice to her Country.

I hope all good Englishmen may feel all good Americans their friends—as for me, be it in peace or war, I shall wish for the good of our race that your Country may withstand every shock, and that our children may see her great and free and offering a refuge to the oppressed from every quarter of the globe.

John Bigelow, RETROSPECTIONS OF AN ACTIVE LIFE

AS THOUGH GOD HAD
FORSAKEN THEM

Although best known for her numerous novels, George Sand was also an active political pamphleteer. The extract that follows is from a letter written to her friend, Socialist Deputy Armand Barbès and refers to her son Maurice's visit to the United States.

January 8, 1862

Maurice is here, working on his notes on America. He understood quickly but quite soundly that this false democracy, while proclaiming equality and liberty, has forgotten just one thing, fraternity, whose absence renders the two other privileges not only sterile but harmful. His somewhat official position as their guest compels him to gloss over certain things tactfully, but his understatements are revealing enough.

The level of American hearts and minds would appear to be still lower than our own, and they lack even the military instinct which, in our country, can work wonders under any flag if the cause is a good one. It is as though God had forsaken them to punish them for the sin of slavery which lives on in their prejudices and in their social customs. . . .

George Sand, CORRESPONDANCE COMPLÈTE

Among the many French translations of Harriet Beecher Stowe's *Uncle Tom's Cabin,* there was one by Léon Pilatte for which George Sand wrote the preface. Here, briefly, is her opinion of "the little woman that wrote the book that made this great war," as Mr. Lincoln so succinctly put it when he met Mrs. Stowe early in 1863.

This touching relationship between the slave and his master's child bears witness to a state of affairs that is quite unknown among us. It is the protest of the master himself against the reality of slavery, during the entire period of his life when his soul belongs to God alone. Society seizes hold of him later, the law drives God from him and selfish interests supersede moral consciousness. Upon attaining manhood, the child ceases to be a man and becomes a master. God no longer dwells in his heart. . . .

Mrs. Stowe possesses the true Christian spirit. Her religious fervor glorifies martyrdom but it denies man the right to perpetuate it either by custom or by law. She condemns an interpretation of the Scriptures which tolerates the iniquities of the oppressors. . . . She calls on God himself as witness, she threatens in His name. She shows us the law on one side, man and God on the other. . . . All honor and respect to you, Mrs. Stowe! One day your reward which is graven on heavenly records will also be of this world.

I cannot say she has talent as one understands it in the world of letters, but she has genius, as humanity feels the need of genius—the genius of goodness, not that of the man of letters but of the saint. Yes, a saint!

Preface to UNCLE TOM'S CABIN

A VIEW FROM
PENNSYLVANIA AVENUE

Edward Dicey was one of the few members of the British upper class whose sympathies were with the North. He came to America in 1862 for the *Spectator* and spent six months traveling extensively throughout the Union.

From the windows of my lodgings, I looked out upon the mile-long Pennsylvania Avenue, leading from the broad Potomac River, by the marble palace of the President's, to the snow-white Capitol, and every hour of the day almost I was disturbed while writing by the sound of some military band, as regiment after regiment passed, marching southwards.

Surely no nation in the world has gone through

such a baptism of war as the people of the United States underwent in one short year's time. With the men of the Revolution the memories of the Revolutionary War had died out. Two generations had passed away to whom war was little more than a name. The Mexican campaign was rather a military demonstration than an actual war, and the sixteen years which had elapsed since its termination form a long period in the life of a nation whose whole existence has not completed its first century. Twenty months ago there were not more than 12,000 soldiers in a country of 31,000,000. Almost in a day this state of things passed away. Our English critics were so fond of repeating what the North could not do—how it could not fight, nor raise money, nor conquer the South—that they omitted to mention what the North *had* done. There was no need to go farther than my windows at Washington to see the immensity of the war. . . .

One thing is certain, that there is no physical degeneracy about a race which could produce such regiments as those which formed the army of the Potomac. Men of high stature and burly frames were rare, except in the Kentucky troops; but on the other hand, small, stunted men were almost unknown. I have seen the armies of most European countries; and I have no hesitation in saying that, as far as the average raw material of the rank and file is concerned, the American army is the finest. The officers are, undoubtedly, the weak point of the system. They have not the military air, the self-possession which long habit of command alone can give; while the footing of equality on which they inevitably stand with the volunteer privates deprives them of the *esprit du corps* belonging to a ruling class. Still they are active, energetic, and constantly with their troops. Wonderfully well equipped, too, at this period of the war, were both officers and men. Their clothing was substantial and fitted easily, their arms were good, and the military arrangements were as perfect as money alone could make them. It was remarkable to me how rapidly the new recruits fell into the habits of military service. I have seen a Pennsylvania regiment, raised chiefly from the mechanics of Philadelphia, which, six weeks after its formation was, in my eyes, equal to the average of our best-trained volunteer corps, as far as marching and drill exercise went. At the scene of war itself, there was no playing at soldiering. No gaudy uniforms or crack companies, no distinction of classes. From every part of the North; from the ports of New York and Boston; from the homesteads of New England; from the mines of Pennsylvania and the factories of Pittsburgh; from the shores of the Great Lakes; from the Mississippi valley; and from the faraway Texan prairies these men had come to fight for the Union. It is idle to talk of their being attracted by the pay alone. Large as it is, the pay of thirteen dollars a month is only two dollars more than the ordinary pay of privates in the Federal army during peace times. It is false, moreover, to assert, as the opponents of the North are fond of doing, that the Federal armies were composed exclusively, or even principally, of foreigners. Judging from my own observation, I would say that the percentage of foreigners amongst the privates of the army of the Potomac was barely ten per cent. But in the West, which is almost peopled with Germans, foreigners are, probably, in the majority.

Of course, wherever there is an army, the scum of the population will always be gathered together;

but the average morale and character of the couple of hundred thousand troops collected round Washington was extremely good. There was very little outward drunkenness, and less brawling about the streets than if half a dozen English militia regiments had been quartered there. The number of papers purchased daily by the common soldiers and the amount of letters which they sent through the military post was astonishing to a foreigner, though less strange when you considered that every man in that army, with the exception of a few recent immigrants, could both read and write.

All day and every day while I resided at Washington, the scene before my eyes was one of war. An endless military panorama seemed to be unrolling itself ceaselessly. If you went up to any high point in the city whence you could look over the surrounding country, every hillside seemed covered with camps. The white tents caught your eye on all sides; and across the river the great army of the Potomac stretched miles away, right up to the advanced posts of the Confederates, south of the far-famed Manassas.

Try to realize all this, and then picture to yourself what its effect, seen in fact, and not portrayed by feeble description, must be upon a nation unused to war. The wonder to me is that the American people were not more intoxicated with the consciousness of their newborn strength.

Edward Dicey, SIX MONTHS IN THE FEDERAL STATES

"I AM IN A MINORITY"

Endowed with an enormous range of talents and interests, Richard Monckton Milnes, the first Baron Houghton, was one of those gifted men who turned up with great regularity in the English aristocracy. A poet in his own right, he was a friend of such literary giants as Swinburne, Thackeray, de Tocqueville and Heine. He was probably the first champion of Keats as an important poet and was the first to write a biography of him. Young Henry Adams mentions Milnes frequently in *The Education of Henry Adams*. The contradictory nature of this remarkable man is clearly revealed by the fact that he was a great collector of pornography and at the same time was an early suitor of Florence Nightingale. As a member of Parliament he stood out as a staunch defender of the North when all of the aristocracy was for the South. In a letter to Ambassador Charles F. Adams, written on January 10, 1862, he wrote: "I never could agree with those English politicians who had persuaded themselves that Mr. Seward desired to drive this country into hostilities with yours, and who formed their opinions on this foregone conclusion. I watch the proceedings of your arms and politics with equal interest and earnestly desire the success of both." The following excerpts are from letters to two of his lifelong friends, C. J. MacCarthy and George von Bunsen. MacCarthy, a nephew of the Catholic Archbishop of Westminster, had prepared for the church but left it to enter public service as the Governor of Ceylon. George von Bunsen was the son of the German Ambassador to England.

To C. J. MacCarthy:

January 20, 1862

I am in a minority of two or three, in the House of Commons and society being all Southern. . . .

To George von Bunsen:

February 6, 1862

Parliament meets today, with no great prospect of change of any kind. The feeling about America is intensely Southern, and I, with my Northern sympathies, remain in greater isolation than ever. The manufacturing districts are behaving very well, doing nothing to urge the Government to break the blockade, feeling, I suspect, that it is by no means certain whether the further complications which should be induced might not make things still worse.

To C. J. MacCarthy:

September, 1862

The Americans told Mr. Trollope, "Sir, we are a recuperative people." (They need it now, poor fellows!). . . . As to general politics, Lord Palmerston's digestion is excellent, and thus England is comfortable in the midst of the cotton famine, which only starves a few thousand operatives, who are patiently passing away. . . .

To C. J. MacCarthy:

October, 1862

The distress in the cotton districts is frightful, and is a sad example of the want of prevision in the wealth-makers of England. Even now I don't understand why British capital has not run off with all the Indian cotton and left the Hindoos naked. . . . The manufacturers, for their part, have no notion of being ruined, along with their artisans. They have made their own wealth, not inherited it; and have no notion of looking on it as a trust, but as their own, which they can do what they like with. It will thus require very fine language indeed to get much out of their pockets, and I doubt whether even Gladstone could do it. For my part, I see no gleam of good in anything American. The lower civilization as represented by the South is much braver and cunninger and daringer than the cultivated shopkeepers of the North. It is just as if the younger sons of the Irish and Scotch nobility were turned loose against the *bourgeoisie* of Leeds. They would kill the men and run away with the women and fire the houses before the respectables knew where they were, or had learned the goosestep. And then the rebels will found such a jolly republic, with little work, and plenty of quadroons and everything pleasant. I shall not be surprised to see the slave trade going briskly before you and I retire. . . .

To C. J. MacCarthy:

June, 1863

The American affair gets worse, the French strongly pressing recognition of the South. I shall oppose it to the last, whether brought forward by this or any other Government. . . .

T. Wemyss Reid, THE LIFE, LETTERS AND FRIENDSHIPS OF RICHARD MONCKTON MILNES

"YOU POOR MAD THINGS—
WHAT WILL BECOME OF YOU?"

John Ruskin, author, art critic and political economist, engaged in extensive correspondence with his fellow scholar in America, Charles Eliot Norton. Norton, besides teaching the history of art at Harvard, was co-editor with James Russell Lowell of the *North American Review* and later was one of the founders of the *Nation*. We shall hear from Mr. Ruskin again later on.

Mornex, Haute Savoie, shortest day, February, 1862

. . . Your horrid war troubles anger me sometimes. The roar of it seems to clang in the blue sky. You poor mad things—what will become of you?

Ever affectionately yours,
J. Ruskin.

Mornex, Haute Savoie, August 28, 1862

. . . As for your American War, I still say as I said at first—if they want to fight, they deserve to fight and suffer. It is entirely horrible and abominable, but nothing else will do. Do you remember Mrs. Browning's curse on America [a poem denouncing slavery]? I said at the time "She had no business to curse any country but her own," but she, as it appeared afterward, was dying, and knew better than I against whom her words were to be recorded. . . . We have come in for a proper share of suffering —but the strangest thing is how many innocent suffer, while the guiltiest—Derby and D'Israeli and such like—are shooting grouse.

Ever your affectionate,
J. Ruskin.

Cook and Wedderburn, eds., LETTERS OF JOHN RUSKIN

"TO MY AMERICAN FRIENDS..."

Fredrika Bremer retained an active interest in American affairs until her death in 1865. Though fluent in English, Miss Bremer was not always accurate as can be seen in the following letter dated March 30, 1862, which was published in the New York *Daily Tribune.*

. . . You know it well, my friends, without my saying it, what a deep interest I have taken in your present civil strife. But you cannot know how bitterly I have felt to see a bloody, fratricide war pollute a country gifted beyond all others with all the blessings of this earth, a country of which men such as *Horace Mann* and *A. J. Downing,* (each in his way) have worked to make (as God seems to have intended it to be, a paradisi(a)cal home for mankind, a land whose richness of life and beauty recently made a young frensh [sic] traveller Maurice Sand, son of the celebrated frensh[sic]Authoresse George Sand, (Mme. Dudevant) exclaim: "How can people go on killing in a land so full of beauty? This is a country for poets and lovers of nature!"

Signe A. Rooth, SEERESS OF THE NORTHLAND

THE CATHOLIC CHURCH
DEPLORES SLAVERY

Monsignor Dupanloup, Bishop of Orléans, was a member of the French Academy and became Canon of Notre Dame. The following is part of a letter addressed to the clergy in his diocese.

Orléans, April 6, 1862

. . . Slavery has never prepared any man for freedom. On the contrary, the longer it lasts, the more oppressive it becomes. You refuse to set the slaves free under pretext that they are unfit for freedom; and I say to you that this unfitness is fostered and even created by the state of bondage in which they are left to stagnate. Slavery as it exists today has both an abominable origin and terrible consequences. Its origin is the slave trade, condemned by Pope Pius II in 1482, by Pope Paul III in 1557, by Urban VIII in 1639, by Pope Benedict XIV in 1741 and by Pope Grégory XVI in 1839. Its consequence is the destruction of family life and the destruction of freedom, not only the slave's but the master's as well (he is even forbidden to teach his slave how to read!).

Religion may alleviate the suffering of the poor slave by softening the heart of his master; but religion can only deplore a situation which maintains men in the most barbarous state of inferiority. We, priests of God, are duty bound to preach the Gospel to condemned prisoners, to live with convicts, to evangelize the feeble-minded, to dress the wounds of the sick; it is also our mission to console slaves, indeed, we love them, and they love us; but we abhor slavery. I admire the bishops and the priests who live in countries where slavery exists. I appeal to them, to their heart, to their conscience, to their sense of dignity, to the sacred character of their priesthood. They suffer because they know, just as well as I do, that our religion is a religion of free men.

I am aware that to carry out such a mission [the abolition of slavery] is perhaps much more difficult, more arduous than it appears to be, and that it requires time. The masters must receive compensation for their loss; the slaves must be educated, civilized; I know that there can be found among the masters— God forbid that I should accuse them too severely—

men of good faith, honest men and even charitable men. They did not create this situation, they regret it, they deserve an indemnity; and it is already being offered them. Then, too, when the slaves are set free, they will have to learn how to live in society and their bondage has certainly not made them ready for life in a free community. But the priests of Jesus and all good Christians will undertake to teach them all they need to know. . . .

Comte de Montalembert, LA VICTOIRE DU NORD AUX ETATS-UNIS

DEATH UNDER A ROSE BUSH

The Prince de Joinville came to America in 1861 accompanied by his son, the duc de Penthièvre and his two nephews, the comte de Paris and the duc de Chartres. These four French noblemen became interested in the New York 55th, a regiment composed almost entirely of foreigners, a great majority of them French. Eventually, however, they were attached to General McClellan's general staff with the rank of captain. Here follows a glimpse of Prince de Joinville's impressions of the Battle of Fair Oaks, which took place in late May of 1862. And, like all the other European observers and

participants, the Prince offers some
opinions as to how the struggle should
be resolved.

On both sides the men fought with ferocious energy,
without a sound, without a word; when the pressure
became too great, the bayonets went into action. The
artillery, posted some distance to the rear in the
clearings, was firing shells over the heads of the combatants. How I should have liked for all those who
had given their unsparing support to the slaveowners
to be forced to witness this fratricidal struggle! As
punishment, I should like for them to be confronted
with the spectacle of this horrible battlefield on which
thousands of dead and dying lay heaped one upon
the other. I should have liked for them to see the
makeshift field hospitals which had been set up in
the few remaining houses. What terrible misery, what
suffering everywhere! The wounded lay huddled together on the ground, silent, motionless in the unbearable heat of a sunny June day. Here and there a
man, mustering all his remaining strength, would
crawl in search of a bit of shade. I shall never forget
standing and talking with a friend, enjoying the per-
fume of some nearby rose bushes when my friend
suddenly pointed to one of those poor wretches who
had just breathed his last under those very bushes. . . .

Newsboys were hawking the latest editions of the
New York papers on the battlefield itself while the
battle was in progress, and they found people from
both camps eager to buy. . . .

I have noted both my favorable and unfavorable
impressions with an identical frankness. I was sin-

cerely impressed by the good I saw and the evil in no way diminished the friendliness of my feeling toward the American people. . . . I cannot predict what the future will bring, but one thing I do see clearly: Even if the North were to be beaten . . . I should continue to believe in the possibility of reviving the Union; but then its revival could only be accomplished through the triumphant rehabilitation of slavery. If the federal bond were to be broken between the North and the South, the various Northern states would soon follow suit and also disband. Each state would then pursue its own selfish interests and meanwhile the powerful bond of slavery would knit the states of the Southern Confederacy more and more closely together. If the South were to win . . . all of the trade outlets of the Western states would be in the hands of the Confederacy, while the New England states, where the Puritan spirit is still strong and where slavery is sincerely considered a major evil, would find themselves isolated from the rest of the country and forced to depend for a livelihood on the products of their agriculture and on the enterprising spirit and resourcefulness of their large and active seafaring population. . . .

The slave-owning aristocracy would have won its spurs, and having once experienced the intoxication of military prestige, nothing could hold it back. . . .

Great things can be accomplished with the aid of slavery: fabulous wealth can be acquired in a very short time. . . . While the Negro cultivates the land, the entire free population can be mobilized, and with an army favored by such circumstances, victorious battles can be fought against great odds. This is exactly what is happening in Virginia. But such an effort can only be short-lived, for, in the long run, slavery depletes, ruins, demoralizes everything it touches.

Prince de Joinville, GUERRE D'AMERIQUE—CAMPAGNE DE POTOMAC

BRITAIN COMES TO THE DEFENSE

OF SOUTHERN WOMANHOOD

After the surrender of New Orleans on April 25, 1862, General Benjamin Franklin Butler, or "Beast Butler" as he was called by the Southerners, became military governor of the city. Ardently loyal Southern ladies manifested their patriotism by spitting upon Union soldiers whenever they appeared on the streets. For a while this unladylike behavior continued and the Northern soldiers took their abuse like gentlemen until General Butler issued his famous order authorizing Federal troops to treat as "Women of the town" those women who publicly insulted Northern troops. The British press promptly interpreted the order as an incitement to commit rape and other assorted atrocities on the flower of Southern womanhood. Lord Palmerston expressed his horror in a letter to American Ambassador Charles F. Adams.

Brockett, *11 June, 1862*
Confidential

My Dear Sir: I cannot refrain from taking the liberty of saying to you that it is difficult if not impossible to express adequately the disgust which must be excited in the mind of every honorable man by the general order of General Butler given in the inclosed extract from yesterday's *Times*. Even when a town is taken by assault it is the practice of the Commander of the conquering army to protect to his utmost the inhabitants and especially the female part of them, and I will venture to say that no example can be found in the history of civilized nations till the publication of this order, of a general guilty in cold blood of so infamous an act as deliberately to hand over the female inhabitants of a conquered city to the unbridled license of an unrestrained soldiery.

If the Federal Government chuses [sic] to be served by men capable of such revolting outrages, they must submit to abide by the deserved opinion which mankind will form of their conduct. My dear sir, yours faithfully,

Palmerston.

PROCEEDINGS OF THE MASSACHUSETTS HISTORICAL SOCIETY

In an effort to tone down the effects of this letter, Lord Russell, Palmerston's

Foreign Secretary, suggested the following in a letter to Palmerston:

June 13, 1862

Adams has been here in a dreadful state about the letter you have written him about Butler.

I declined to give him my opinion and asked him to do nothing more until I had seen or written to you.

What you say of Butler is true enough, tho' he denies your interpretation of the order.

But it is not clear that the President approves of the order, and I think if you could add something to the effect that you respect the Government of President Lincoln, and do not wish to impute to them the fault of Butler, it might soothe him. If you could withdraw the letter altogether it would be the best. But this you may not like to do.

E. D. Adams, GREAT BRITAIN AND THE AMERICAN CIVIL WAR

THE BALL OPENS

Heros von Borcke was a Prussian aristocrat who had made a gallant career for himself in various European armies as a professional soldier. The influence of his breeding and background naturally made him gravitate toward the Confederate cause and he managed to run the blockade and join General Jeb Stuart's forces as Chief of Staff early in June, 1862. Perhaps because they had so much in common— a flair for colorful uniforms, a romantic response to the sights and sounds of war, actually a feeling that warfare in itself was a manly and heroic pursuit—that an immediate and deep bond sprang up between the two men. In his book, *Memoirs of the Confederate War for Independence,* von Borcke managed to distill the horrors of war with a pageantry and color that make it extremely lively reading.

Summer, 1862—Accustomed as I was to European discipline and uniform, I must confess that on me the first impression of these Confederate soldiers was not favourable, and far was I from any idea how soon these same men would excite my highest admiration on the battle-field. . . . At the appointed hour I repaired to the War Department and was received with great kindness by General Randolph, a most intelligent and amiable gentleman, who, after I had endeavoured to explain to him my plans and wishes in execrable English, gave me a letter to General J.E.B. Stuart, then commanding the cavalry of the army defending Richmond.

It was no easy matter to find General Stuart who, as commanding officer of the outposts, was anywhere along the extended lines, and the sun was near its setting when we reached the camp of the 1st Virginia Cavalry. Here I presented myself for information to the officer in command, Colonel Fitzhugh Lee, who assured me that it would be next to impossible to find General Stuart that night and kindly offered me the hospitality of his tent. The camp was a novelty to me in the art of castrametation. The horses were not picketed in regular lines as in European armies, but were scattered about anywhere in the neighbouring wood, some tethered to swinging limbs, some tied to small trees, others again left to browse at will upon the undergrowth. In a very short time I was perfectly at home in the Colonel's tent, where the officers of his regiment had assembled, and where the lively strains of the banjo alternated with patriotic songs and animated discourse. During the evening a supper was served which, under existing circumstances, was really luxurious, and one of the chief dishes of which consisted of the eggs of terrapin found in a creek near the camp by Colonel Lee's faithful Negro servant, who was at once head-cook, valet and steward. I am sure that no work of art from the kitchen of the Café Riche could have been more gratifying to my hungry appetite than these terrapin's eggs taken out of a Virginia swamp and cooked upon the instant in a cavalry encampment.

I was awake and fully dressed the next morning when Colonel Lee informed me he had just received marching orders. He added that my best chance of meeting General Stuart was to ride with the regiment. It was marvellous to see how readily these unmilitary-looking troopers obeyed the orders of their colonel, and with what discipline and rapidity the breaking up of the camp was managed. The men were all Virginians, whose easy and graceful seat betrayed the constant habit of horse-back exercise and they were mounted mostly on blooded animals, some which the most ambitious Guardsman or the most particular "swell" in London would have been glad to show off in Hyde Park. After a ride of three hours, passing directly through Richmond to the opposite side of the city, we reached our destination and Colonel Lee pointed out to me a man, galloping rapidly along on an active, handsome horse. This was Stuart, the man whose arrival I awaited so anxiously, and who subsequently became one of the truest and best friends I have had in this world.

General Stuart was a stoutly built man, rather above the middle height, of a most frank and winning expression, the lower part of his fine face covered with a thick brown beard, which flowed over his breast. His eye was quick and piercing, of a light blue in repose, but changing to a darker tinge under high excitement. His whole person seemed instinct with vitality, and altogether he was to me the model of a dashing cavalry leader. Stuart had passed nearly all his waking hours in the saddle and thus became one of the most fearless and dexterous horsemen in America, and he had acquired a love of adventure which made activity a necessity of his being. He delighted in the neighing of the charger and the clangour of the bugle, and he had something of Murat's weakness for the vanities of military parade. He betrayed this latter quality in his jaunty uniform, which consisted of a small grey jacket, trousers of the same stuff, and over them high military boots, a yellow silk sash, and a grey slouch hat, surmounted by a sweeping black ostrich plume. Thus attired, sitting gracefully on his fine horse, he did not fail to attract the notice and admiration of all who saw him ride along.

At the moment of our first meeting we could exchange but a few words. The battle was just about to commence and my presentation to him was necessarily hurried and informal. After reading General Randolph's letter, he said he should be glad to have me at his side during the day's fight, and then presented me to a number of well-mounted young officers, members of his Staff, and to General Longstreet and his suite. At this instant the roar of the artillery gave the signal that the "ball had opened," and the whole cavalcade, the generals leading, proceeded in rapid gallop to the front.

Heros von Borcke,
MEMOIRS OF THE CONFEDERATE WAR FOR INDEPENDENCE

ORIGIN OF A CLASSIC

Les Miserables was widely read by the soldiers of both armies. A cheap, pirated edition, called the "Volunteers' Edition," was published in America. The soldiers carried the book in their knapsacks and read it eagerly between battles. They would call each other by the names of the leading characters in the book. In the gruelling winter of 1864–1865 the men in General Lee's army nicknamed themselves *Lee's Miserables*. The following is an excerpt from a letter to Lamartine in which Hugo explains his purpose in writing the famous classic.

June 24, 1862

Every man a property owner, and none a master, this for me is true social and political economy. . . . Insofar as man may express his will, I seek to do away with human fatality, I condemn slavery, I banish poverty, I instruct ignorance, I heal sickness, I lighten darkness, I hate hatred. This is where I stand and this is why I wrote *Les Miserables.*

COMPLETE WORKS OF VICTOR HUGO

THE CONTINENT DIVIDED IS INCONCEIVABLE

The following letter from the comte de Paris was addressed to François Buloz, editor of *Revue des Deux Mondes.* The letter has never been published and was in the possession of M. Boucher, a professor at Chatellerault College in France. M. Boucher has put this and other unpublished

comte de Paris letters at the disposal
of Mr. Alfred Krebs, a French historian engaged in a study of Franco-
American relations and it is through
the kindness of Mr. Krebs that this
letter is published for the first time
anywhere.

July 29, 1862

Unfortunately for the world at large the chances of
a rapid solution of the conflict are becoming more
and more remote. These delays are certainly to be
deplored, but one must try to analyze their true
meaning, and I really cannot understand the illusions
of those Europeans who rejoice at the defeat of the
Federal government. Their most cherished dream,
the continent divided into two republics, founded
each upon two diametrically opposed social principles
and prospering peacefully side by side, is just as inconceivable now as it was before the lifting of the
Richmond siege. The North, far from giving way to
discouragement, will be spurred on to new efforts,
and the South will have gained a measure of confidence in itself which will ruin every hope of quick
reconciliation.

Both parties are fighting for their very existence, as
well as for the supremacy of the principle upon which
they are founded. The South, in a tragic impulse,
took up arms because the North refused to lend itself
any longer to the extension of slavery. If this new
state founded on slavery is to hold its own against the
neighboring free states, which had, until secession,
given moral support to the slave-owners, then the

Confederacy must comprise all the slave states actually in existence and enough additional territory to be able to extend its influence. This the North cannot accept without condemning itself to death. On the social plane slavery, especially in temperate climates such as exist in the Border States, puts an end to all possibilities of progress. It impedes the development of free labor and emigration far more efficiently than do mountains or deserts.

Everywhere you hear people saying that the restoration of the Union is impossible. But what seems even more impossible is the setting up of a Secessionist Confederation. The South would have to win many more battles than the North in order to establish its superiority. Industry, intelligence, wealth, the force of numbers and the moral strength derived from fighting against slavery are all on the side of the North. Hard blows were dealt the Northerners and because of their inexperience they will certainly receive more hard blows in the future, but they can return them and seem to want to return them. After all, the Virginia campaign this spring was far from a defeat. . . . The fortunes of war can very well turn in favor of the Federal army in September and it may attain the success it was on the point of winning last month. As far as I am concerned, I hope for its victory as strongly as when I was fighting in its ranks. To me it would mean the just reward due a young and liberal nation defending its institutions and its very existence.

MARX-ENGELS

CORRESPONDENCE CONTINUED

Engels to Marx:

July 30, 1862

Things go wrong in America. . . . What cowardice in government and Congress! They are afraid of conscription, of resolute financial steps, of attacks on slavery, of everything that is urgently necessary; they let everything loaf along as it will, and if the semblance of some measure finally gets through Congress, the honorable Lincoln so qualifies it that nothing at all is left of it any longer. This slackness, this collapse like a punctured pig's bladder, under the pressure of defeats that have annihilated one army, the strongest and best, and actually left Washington exposed, this total absence of any elasticity in the whole mass of the people—this proves to me that it is all up. . . .

For the South, on the contrary—it's no use shutting one's eyes to the fact—it's a matter of bloody earnest. That we get no cotton is already one proof. The guerrillas in the border states are a second. But that after being thus shut off from the world, an agricultural people can sustain such a war and after severe defeats and losses in resources, men and territory, can nevertheless now stand forth as the victor and threaten to carry its offensive right into the North, this is in my opinion decisive. . . . If the North does not proceed forthwith in revolutionary fashion, it will get an ungodly hiding and deserve it—and it looks like it.

Marx to Engels:

August 7, 1862

I do not altogether share your views on the American Civil War. I do not think that all is up. . . . The Southerners . . . acted as one man from the beginning. The North itself has turned the slaves into a military force on the side of the Southerners, instead of turning it against them. The South leaves productive labor to the slaves and could therefore put its whole fighting strength in the field without disturbance. The South had unified military leadership, the North had not. . . . In my opinion all this will take another turn. In the end the North will make war seriously, adopt revolutionary methods and throw over the domination of the border slave statesmen. . . . The Northwest and New England wish to and will force the government to give up the diplomatic method of conducting war which it has used hitherto. . . . If Lincoln does not give way (which he will do, however) there will be a revolution.

The long and short of the business seems to me to be that a war of this kind must be conducted on revolutionary lines, while the Yankees have so far been trying to conduct it constitutionally.

Marx to Engels:

September 10, 1862

As regards the Yankees, I am assuredly still of my previous opinion that the North will finally prevail; certainly the Civil War may go through all sorts of episodes, even armistices, perhaps, and be long drawn out. . . .

The manner in which the North wages war is only to be expected from a *bourgeois* republic, where fraud has so long reigned supreme. The South, an oligarchy, is better adapted thereto, particularly as it is an oligarchy where the whole of the productive labor falls on the Negroes and the four millions of "white trash" are filibusters by profession. All the same, I would wager my head that these boys come off second best, despite "Stonewall Jackson." To be sure, it is possible that it will come to a sort of revolution in the North itself first. . . . It seems to me that you let yourself be swayed a little too much by the military aspect of things.

Marx and Engels, THE CIVIL WAR IN THE UNITED STATES

TEXAS FOR BARTER

Leaders of the Confederacy, thrashing about desperately to secure European intervention on their side and at any cost, expressed themselves in no uncertain terms as to the alternative they would prefer to a Northern victory. William Howard Russell reported to the London *Times:*

. . . Then cropped out again the expression of regret for the rebellion of 1776, and the desire that if it came to the worst, England would receive back her erring children, or give them a prince under whom they could secure a monarchial form of Government. There is no doubt about the earnestness with which these things are said. . . .

Texas, for example, became negotiable property in order to gain foreign support. A Monsieur B. Theron, who represented both France and Spain as consul in Galveston, wrote the following letter to Governor F. R. Lubbock of Texas. The consul was expelled by the Governor for his efforts.

August 18, 1862

Sir:

Will you be kind enough to inform me *confidentially* of your personal opinion on the following questions.

1st. The annexation of the Republic of Texas to the United States was or was not a good political measure?

2nd. The act of disunion and of the junction of the State of Texas to the Southern States was or was not another good or bad politic taken by the State?

3rd. The re-establishment of the old republic of Texas will or will not be beneficial to our beloved adopted country?

Your answer to the questions, Sir, will serve me as a guide in my political correspondence with the governments which I have the honor to represent. . . .

DIPLOMATIC CORRESPONDENCE, 1863-1864

Based on reports from Mexico, a Vienna newspaper on September 21, 1863, interpreted the Confederate-French dealings to suit Austrian purposes of the political moment.

The French Government is supposed to have arranged with the American Southern States for the cession of

Texas. It is confidently assumed that the overwhelmingly German population of Texas would readily submit themselves to a German Prince. It is apparently not feared that in consequence of this cession a war would arise between France and North America. Should, however, the North of America, besides the still continuing contest with the Confederates, be willing to burden themselves with such a war in addition, then France would not object, perhaps even wish for it, in order at least to be able to interfere with armed force in favor of the South.

> At the end of December, 1863, Drouyn de Lhuys, Foreign Minister of France, assured the American Minister William Dayton:

France would not take Texas as a gift, even if it were accompanied with a handsome bribe besides.

DIPLOMATIC CORRESPONDENCE, 1864-1865

THE EFFECTS OF INTERVENTION

> Edouard Laboulaye was a professor of jurisprudence at the Collège de France and a member of the Institut de France. In addition to works on

French and Roman law, he was the author of a political history of the United States. The following article first appeared in the *Journal des Debats*, August, 1862.

While the North was making such spirited preparations for the war, what was the South about? What prevented the South from competing with the North for the sympathy of Europe? If the tariff was the true origin of the war, and the supremacy of the North the only fear of the planters, a fairer occasion could not have presented itself for throwing overboard the fatal clog of slavery. Let somebody publish a program of what the South proposes to do; that is the way to bring round public opinion. Let not the South delude herself. Her soldiers are brave, her diplomatists adroit. She is keeping back the cotton of which Europe has a pressing need; she is flattering certain political jealousies by predicting the approaching dismemberment of the United States; but notwithstanding all chances in her favor, the South will be deceived in the object of her ambition. . . . To succeed, the South must have the help of Europe, and this help she will not have. Whatever may be the sufferings of the manufacturing classes, and whatever the schemes of diplomatists, there is one fact which towers above everything else, and that is—SLAVERY. This is the feeling of Europe, and the knowledge of this feeling will hold back more than one government. . . .

France has a twofold interest at stake in America: a commercial interest and a political interest.

The scarcity of cotton reduces to misery great masses of laborers. Whence came this scarcity? Is it the fault of the North? No; the North, notwithstanding the war, is willing to buy cotton from the insurgents and sell it to Europe. But the South has perceived from the first that it could not gain its point, except with the support of Europe; it has calculated on getting this help at last, though at a hard bargain perhaps, by starving us. To induce Europe to intervene, in spite of herself, is the hope and the policy of the Confederates.

What means is there of obtaining cotton if the South persists in this selfish course which costs us so dear? There is but one, and that is the end of the war. The end of the war may come in a natural way, or it may be decided by the intervention of Europe. Of these two ways the second is the more dangerous and the less sure.

To intervene would be to excite on the one side the hopes, on the other the anger of two infuriated parties; it would be to add fuel to a flame which may set the whole world on fire. These are those uneasy and restless people who propose to us *not to intervene, but to recognize the South*. But will this recognition procure us cotton? No; it will not give us the right to break the blockade, and so it will not end the war. What will it gain for us? Nothing, but the loss of that position of mediators and friends, which at a favorable moment might enable us to put an end to the conflict. To recognize the South is to give it our moral support, is to declare in advance that its pretensions are lawful, to take sides and therefore to abandon the position of possible arbitrators. Of what use to us will be this measure, which will offend the North and put our future in jeopardy?

But let us suppose that the North . . . allows us to regulate the dismemberment of America—all impossible suppositions, when you remember that we are speaking of a youthful, ardent and patriotic people, a people which has been a year under arms—when we shall have succeeded in this gigantic enterprise, what have we done? We shall have belied all our political traditions, we shall have weakened France and strengthened England, while crushing our most useful and most faithful allies! These political interests are more important than the interests of our manufactures; and yet some appear to forget this fact, or to wink it out of sight, whenever it is convenient for their purposes.

What, in fact, would be the effect of the dismemberment of America, but the weakening and the destruction of the United States navy to the advantage of the English navy? England acts on the principle that its navy ought always to be twice as powerful as ours, which is the same as saying that the English choose always to be in a condition to cope with confederated Europe. To dismember America is the same thing as restoring the empire of the seas to our rivals; and to maintain the unity of America is to maintain liberty on the ocean and the peace of the world.

Edouard Laboulaye, "THE UNITED STATES AND FRANCE"

EUROPE HAS BEEN

MOST PROFOUNDLY DECEIVED

In the spring of 1838 Alfred de Vigny, the great French poet, novelist and playwright, met a young American woman, Julia Battlegang, from Charleston, Virginia, who was living in Paris with her family. Julia became the poet's mistress. When the Battlegang family returned to the United States the lovers kept up a close correspondence for many years. After the outbreak of war the recurrent theme of Julia's letters to Vigny was her intense hatred of the Yankees. The poet, who died in 1863, wrote Julia begging her to seek refuge in French Martinique or English Jamaica, "there to await safely for the outcome of this most terrible drama, for the issue of this cruel war now being waged against you." This letter first appeared in an article, "Vigny and the Yankees," by Henri Guillemin, published in *Le Monde*, March 5, 1955.

September 10, 1862

. . . Those abominable acts of cruelty perpetrated by the Northerners in New Orleans remind one of the invasion of the Barbarians, of Attila's Huns or even worse, of the Vandals. I well understand your hatred for those depraved and ferocious men who are drowning in blood the whole of your beloved country.

The heroism shown by your armies is as great as that of Saragossa's defenders at the time of the Spanish War for Independence. Your enemies, meanwhile, have finally rent with their own hands the veil of their hypocrisy. When Lincoln in a public declara-

167

tion admitted that if he could restore the Union without abolishing slavery he would do so, and when he advises a delegation of *free Negroes* to leave the United States for good and go into voluntary exile in Central America where they would be penned up like so much cattle and put to work in the coal mines as slaves—all of this for the simple reason that the sight and the very presence of them happens to be displeasing to the delicate senses of white people! Europe has been most profoundly deceived as to the real motive behind this attitude of the North, which has been consistently posing as the liberator of the black man. O Tartuffe! [Molière's prototype of the religious hypocrite.]

If they want to, let them open and read all our letters and they will see with their own eyes how contemptible they seem to men who are really free and who do not have the misfortune to live under a tyranny which they try to pass under the guise of a true republic, when by doing so they bring shame to the very word republic. A wise state is not one that resorts to brute force, to murder and fire in order to find a solution to the complex problem of states' rights. It is a question that should have been settled in public debate and every important political organization in America should have been called upon to participate in such a debate. The minority would have had to accept the decision of the majority in a friendly and resigned spirit. But the victories your noble cause deserves are already avenging the wrongs that have been done you: yours are all the good generals, all the true heroism among the soldiers, and with you also is the power of this great and generous spirit which rejects hypocrisy and violence.

Henri Guillemin, "VIGNY AND THE YANKEES"

INTERMISSION AT A BALL

Heros von Borcke provides a charming description of wartime entertainment:

We were indulging in the dreamy sentiment natural to the hour, when the gay voice of Stuart broke in— "Major, what a capital place for us to give a ball in honour of our arrival in Maryland! don't you think we could manage it?" To this there was a unanimous response in the affirmative, which was especially hearty on the part of the ladies. It was at once agreed that the ball should be given. I undertook to make all necessary arrangements for the illumination and decoration of the hall, the issuing of the cards of invitation, &c., leaving to Stuart the matter of the music, which he gladly consented to provide.

A soldier's life is so uncertain, and his time is so little at his own disposal, that in affairs of this sort delays are always to be avoided; and so we determined on our way home, to the great joy of our fair companions, that the ball should come off on the following evening.

There was great stir of preparation at headquarters on the morning of the 8th. Invitations to the ball were sent out to all the families in Urbana and its neighbourhood, and to the officers of Hampton's brigade. The large halls of the Academy were aired and swept and festooned with roses, and decorated with battle flags borrowed from the different regiments. At seven in the evening all was complete, and already the broad avenue was filled with our fair guests, proceeding to the scene of festivity according to their social rank and fortune—some on foot, others in simple light "rockaways," others again in stately family coaches, driven by fat Negro coachmen who sat upon the box with great dignity. Very soon the sound of distant bugles announced the coming of the band of the 18th Mississippi Infantry, the Colonel and Staff of the regiment, who had been invited as an act of courtesy, leading the way, and the band playing in excellent style, the well-known air of Dixie. Amid the loud applause of the numerous invited and uninvited guests, we now made our grand *entrée* into the large hall, which was brilliantly lighted with tallow candles.

As master of the ceremonies, it was my office to arrange the order of the different dances, and I had decided upon a polka as the best for an animated beginning. I had selected the New York Rebel as the queen of the festival, and had expected to open the ball with her as my partner, and my surprise was great indeed when my fair friend gracefully eluded my extended arms, and with some confusion explained that she did not join in round dances, thus making me uncomfortably acquainted for the first time with the fact that in America, and especially in the South, young ladies rarely waltz except with brothers or first cousins, and indulge only in reels and contredances with strangers.

Not to be baffled, however, I at once ordered the time of the music to be changed, and had soon forgotten my disappointment as to the polka in a very lively quadrille. Louder and louder sounded the instruments, quicker and quicker moved the dancers, and the whole crowded room, with its many exceedingly pretty women and its martial figures of officers in their best uniforms, presented a most striking spectacle of gaiety and enjoyment.

Suddenly enters an orderly covered with dust, and reports in a loud voice to General Stuart that the enemy have surprised and driven in our pickets and are attacking our camp in force, while at the same moment the sound of shots in rapid succession is distinctly borne to us on the midnight air.

The excitement which followed this announcement I cannot undertake to describe. The music crashed into a *concordia discors*. The officers rushed to their weapons and called for their horses, panic-stricken fathers and mothers endeavoured in a frantic way to collect around them their bewildered children, while the young ladies ran to and fro in most admired despair. General Stuart maintained his accustomed coolness and composure. Our horses were immediately saddled, and in less than five minutes we were in rapid gallop to the front. Upon arriving there we found, as is usually the case in such sudden alarms, that things were by no means so desperate as they had been represented.

Colonel Baker, with the splendid 1st North Carolina regiment, had arrested the bold forward movement of the Yankees. Pelham, with his guns in favourable position, was soon pouring a rapid fire upon their columns. The other regiments of the command were speedily in the saddle. The line of battle having been formed, Stuart gave the order for a general attack, and with great rage and fury we precipitated ourselves upon the foe, who paid with

171

the loss of many killed and wounded and a considerable number of prisoners for their unmannerly interruption of our social amusement. They were pursued in their headlong flight for several miles by the 1st North Carolina, until, a little past midnight, they got quite out of reach, and all was quiet again.

It was about one o'clock in the morning when we got back to the Academy, where we found a great many of our fair guests still assembled, awaiting with breathless anxiety the result of the conflict. As the musicians had never dispersed, General Stuart ordered them again to strike up; many of our pretty fugitives were brought back by young officers who eagerly volunteered for that commendable purpose; and as everybody was determined that the Yankees should not boast of having completely broken up our party, the dancing was resumed in less than half an hour, and kept up till the first glimmer of dawn. At this time the ambulances laden with the wounded of last night's engagement were slowly approaching the Academy, as the only building at Urbana that was at all suited to the purposes of an hospital. Of course the music was immediately stopped and the dancing ceased, and our lovely partners in the quadrille at once became "ministering angels" to the sufferers.

Heros von Borcke,
MEMOIRS OF THE CONFEDERATE WAR FOR INDEPENDENCE

LOOK AT THEIR WILD WAYS...

Original editorial comment was quite rare in the six leading newspapers in Spain at the time of the war. Most of the news was copied from European newspapers reflecting extremely reactionary views of the American struggle. The following is an editorial from *Pensamiento Español,* published in September, 1862.

In the model republic of what *were* the United States, we see more and more clearly of how little account is a society constituted without God, merely for the sake of men. Look at their wild ways of annihilating each other, confiscating each other's goods, mutually destroying each other's cities, and cordially wishing each other extinct! The Federals declare their enemies' slaves free, and the latter refuse to allow Federal regiments of whites and blacks any rights of war. Both muzzle the press; both vie with each other in reprisals; and at the end of a year of war they are both on the road to becoming barbarians. The history of the model republic can be summed up in a few words. It came into being by rebellion. It was founded on atheism. It was populated by the dregs of all the nations in the world. It has lived without law of

God or man. Within a hundred years, greed has ruined it. Now it is fighting like a cannibal, and it will die in a flood of blood and mire. Such is the real history of the one and only state in the world which has succeeded in constituting itself according to the flaming theories of democracy. The example is too horrible to stir any desire for imitation in Europe....

Jordan and Pratt, EUROPE AND THE AMERICAN CIVIL WAR

PALMERSTON AND RUSSELL
CONSIDER MEDIATION

In September of 1862, when the North was being badly beaten by Lee's armies, Viscount Palmerston, Prime Minster of England, exchanged views with his Foreign Secretary, Lord John Russell, on the question of intervention.

94 Piccadilly: September 14, 1862

My dear Russell,—The detailed accounts given in the "Observer" to-day of the battles of August 29 and 30 between the Confederates and the Federals show that the latter got a very complete smashing; and it seems not altogether unlikely that still greater disasters await them, and that even Washington or Baltimore may fall into the hands of the Confederates.

If this should happen, would it not be time for us to consider whether in such a state of things England and France might not address the contending parties and recommend an arrangement upon the basis of separation?

—Yours sincerely,
Palmerston

Gotha: September 17, 1862

My dear Palmerston,—Whether the Federal army is destroyed or not, it is clear that it is driven back to Washington, and has made no progress in subduing the insurgent States. Such being the case, I agree with you that the time is come for offering mediation to the United States Government, with a view to the recognition of the independence of the Confederates. I agree further, that, in case of failure, we ought ourselves to recognise the Southern States as an independent State. For the purpose of taking so important a step, I think we must have a meeting of the Cabinet. The 23rd or 30th would suit me for the meeting.

We ought then, if we agree on such a step, to propose it first to France, and then, on the part of England and France, to Russia and other powers, as a measure decided upon by us.

We ought to make ourselves safe in Canada, not by sending more troops there, but by concentrating those we have in a few defensible posts before the winter sets in.

J. Russell

My dear Russell,—Your plan of proceedings about the mediation between the Federals and Confederates seems to be excellent. Of course, the offer would be made to both the contending parties at the same time; for, though the offer would be as sure to be accepted by the Southerns as was the proposal of the Prince of Wales by the Danish Princess, yet, in the one case as in the other, there are certain forms which it is decent and proper to go through.

A question would occur whether, if the two parties were to accept the mediation, the fact of our mediating would not of itself be tantamount to an acknowledgment of the Confederates as an independent State.

Might it not be well to ask Russia to join England and France in the offer of mediation? . . .

We should be better without her in the mediation, because she would be too favourable to the North; but on the other hand her participation in the offer might render the North more willing to accept it.

The after communication to the other European powers would be quite right, although they would be too many for mediation.

As to the time of making the offer, if France and Russia agree,—and France, we know, is quite ready, and only waiting for our concurrence—events may be taking place which might render it desirable that the offer should be made before the middle of October.

It is evident that a great conflict is taking place to the north-west of Washington, and its issue must have a great effect on the state of affairs. If the Federals sustain a great defeat, they may be at once ready for mediation, and the iron should be struck while it is hot. If, on the other hand, they should have the best of it, we may wait awhile and see what may follow.

Yours sincerely,
Palmerston.

Spencer Walpole, THE LIFE OF LORD JOHN RUSSELL

October 2

My dear Russell,—I return you Granville's letter which contains much deserving of serious consideration. There is no doubt that the offer of Mediation upon the basis of Separation would be accepted by the South. Why should it not be accepted? It would give the South in principle the points for which they are fighting. The refusal, if refusal there was, would come from the North, who would be unwilling to give up the principle for which they have been fighting so long as they had a reasonable expectation that by going on fighting they could carry their point. The condition of things therefore which would be favourable to an offer of mediation would be great success of the South against the North. That state of things seemed ten days ago to be approaching. Its advance has been lately checked, but we do not yet know the real course of recent events, and still less can we foresee what is about to follow. Ten days or a fortnight more may throw a clearer light upon future prospects.

As regards possible resentment on the part of the Northerns following upon acknowledgment of the Independence of the South, it is quite true that we should have less to care about that resentment in the spring when communication with Canada was open, and when our naval force could more easily operate upon the American coast, than in winter when we are cut off from Canada and the American coast is not so safe.

But if the acknowledgment were made at one and the same time by England, France and some other Powers, the Yankees would probably not seek a quarrel with us alone, and would not like one against a European Confederation. Such a quarrel would render certain and permanent that Southern Independence the acknowledgment of which would have caused it.

The first communication to be made by England and France to the contending parties might be, not an absolute offer of mediation but a friendly suggestion whether the time was not come when it might be well for the two parties to consider whether the war, however long continued, could lead to any other result than separation; and whether it might not therefore be best to avoid the great evils which must necessarily flow from a prolongation of hostilities by at once coming to an agreement to treat upon that principle of separation which must apparently be the inevitable result of the contest, however long it may last.

The best thing would be that the two parties should settle details by direct negotiation with each other, though perhaps with rancorous hatred now existing between them this might be difficult. But their quarrels in negotiation would do us no harm if they did not lead to a renewal of war. An armistice, if not accompanied by a cessation of blockades, would be all in favor of the North, especially if New Orleans remained in the hands of the North.

The whole matter is full of difficulty, and can only
be cleared up by some more decided events between
the contending armies.

Palmerston.

E. D. *Adams*, GREAT BRITAIN AND THE AMERICAN CIVIL WAR

"YOUR REVOLUTION IS RIDICULOUS
AND NOT TRAGIC ENOUGH"

Best known in this country as the
author of *Carmen,* the book on which
Bizet based his opera, Prosper Mérimée was a novelist, historian, archae-
ologist and linguist who translated
Pushkin and other Russians into
French. He was a senator during the
Second Empire and prominent at
Court due to his long-standing friendship with Empress Eugenie and her
mother. New editions of his seven-
volume correspondence appear peri-
odically in France and the following
is an excerpt from a letter to his
friend Edward Lee Childe, nephew of
Robert E. Lee. More of M. Mérimée's
derisive comments appear later in this
book.

Your revolution, for it really is a revolution, is entirely modern in character. Its pattern is identical to that of our revolution of 1848, ridiculous and not tragic enough. I refuse to consider as tragic disasters all the battles being fought between your uncle and those fools. What I mean to say is that though you've imitated the waste of our first revolution, you've not imitated its terrifying grandeur; like ourselves in 1848, you've committed a lot of blunders but no crimes. If you had shot or hung your incompetent generals, fired on or drowned the people of New Orleans instead of threatening their women with gentle rape, you would perhaps have done great things as well as abominable ones. It's quite possible, it's even more than probable, that you will come to that point some time soon. Now that the fashion in Europe is to admire the South and predict its victory, I'm beginning to grow interested in the North.

Maurice Parturier, ed., COLLECTED LETTERS OF PROSPER MÉRIMÉE

THE COTTON BURNERS OF AMERICA
AND THE LANCASHIRE SUFFERERS

Peter Sinclair, a Scotsman who resided in the United States for five years, returned to his country embittered by what he considered the treachery of the South in withholding cotton from the Lancashire mills. Thereafter he devoted himself to exposing the behind-the-scenes collusion between British wealth and the Confederacy.

To compel Great Britain to recognise the Slaveholders' Confederacy, it was settled in the councils of the rebels long before the commencement of open hostilities that the tremendous power which the monopoly of the cotton trade gave them should be wielded against Great Britain if she hesitated, or delayed, or refused to accede to the wishes of the Confederate Government, so called. . . .

Thus by cotton burning in the Southern Slave States—by refusing to sell it at the ports opened by the United States' Government, by prohibiting its cultivation, by reducing our operatives to the point of starvation, by the employment of emissaries to stir up discontent and disaffection in the cotton manufacturing districts, by attempting to embroil France and England, and by any other diabolical contrivance that can enter into the human mind, do these cotton burners seek to accomplish their ends. . . .

Again and again I repeat, the blockade has nothing to do with the barbarous conduct of the men who come here seeking to be recognized as a separate and independent people. . . . They don't want the blockade raised that England may get Cotton. No, they want it raised that they may be enabled to carry on the war. . . .

How different the conduct of the United States Government and the Free men of the Free States.

No sooner did the Government succeed in regaining possession of Beaufort, Port Royal, New Orleans, Memphis, Nashville, and the other Cotton Markets, than it made provision for the reopening of the Cotton trade. The Blockade was declared on the 19th of April, 1861. It was removed from the ports of Beaufort in North Carolina, Port Royal in South Carolina, and New Orleans in Louisiana, on the 12th day of May, 1862. Cotton agents accompanied the armies of the North, who were licensed to purchase Cotton, not in these ports, which were open to all, but in the interior of the country, where the humanity of the Government of the United States led them to grant the greatest facilities for procuring the important article of commerce. . . . The United States Government assured the British Government of their anxiety to grant every facility for the obtaining of Cotton, and gave the rebels every facility to sell it. But the result has been what? Simply an order from Jefferson Davis to burn the Cotton to starve the English.

The large amount of British capital invested in sustaining the Southern slaveholders is the main cause of the continuance of the war and therefore the cause of the bloodshed and suffering in America as well as the cause of the terrible suffering in Lancashire in England and Lanarkshire in Scotland. . . .

Score after score of the finest, swiftest British steamers and ships, loaded with British material of war of every description, cannon, rifles by the hundred thousand, powder by the thousands of tons, shot, shell, cartridges, revolvers, swords, etc. with cargo after cargo of army cloths, boots, shoes, blankets, medicines and supplies of every kind, all paid for by British money, at the sole risk of British adventurers, well insured in Lloyd's and under the protection of the British flag, have been sent across the ocean to the insurgents by British agency. To what extent may be judged by the fact that 543 vessels have been seized attempting to break the blockade. All the largest and best of these were British-owned by British subjects and the contents at British risk.

Liverpool has been the headquarters of this British aid of the slave power. Here a wealthy organization exists for the purpose. I only give some faint idea of British complicity in this most disgraceful business. Not that I expect the laws of England or the Government of England will put a stop to it but that the voice of the masses of the British people may be heard on the subject. If they shall condemn it, I shall rejoice that the American people will know that the aid to slavery was not the act of the people of England but only of those men whom the love of gain will lead to enter into any enterprise, however wrong.

How strangely will this conduct contrast with the conduct of the merchants of the Free States, who are seeking to alleviate the sufferings of our manufacturing population by sending us ships loaded with provisions, while we are sending their enemies ships loaded with munitions of war.

Peter Sinclair, "FREEDOM OR SLAVERY IN THE UNITED STATES"

PROPOSALS WILL BE MADE

TO RUSSIA

Vice-Chancellor Prince Gortchakov re-
assures Bayard Taylor, American
Chargé d'Affaires in Russia, in October, 1862:

Your situation is getting worse and worse. The
chances of preserving the Union are growing more
and more desperate. . . . Can you find no basis of
agreement before your strength is so exhausted that
you must lose for many years to come your position
in the world? . . . It is not that alone, but the fury
which seems to possess both sides—the growth of
enmities which are making the gulf continually wider
between the two sections. The hope of their reunion
is growing less and less, and I wish you to impress on
your government that the separation which I fear
must come, will be considered by Russia as one of
great possible misfortune. Russia alone has stood by
you from the very first, and will continue to stand by
you. We are very, *very* anxious that some means
should be adopted, and that *any* course should be
pursued which will prevent the division that now
seems inevitable. One separation will be followed by

another; you will break into fragments. You know the sentiments of Russia! We desire, above all things, the maintenance of the American Union as one indivisible nation. . . . Russia has declared her position and will maintain it. There will be no proposals for intervention. We believe that intervention would do no good at the present. *Proposals will be made to Russia to join in some plan of interference.* She will refuse any invitation of the kind. Russia will occupy the same ground as at the beginning of the struggle. *You may rely upon it, she will not change.* But we entreat you to settle the difficulty. I cannot express to you how profound an anxiety we feel—how serious are our fears.

E. A. Adamov,
"RUSSIA AND THE UNITED STATES AT THE TIME OF THE CIVIL WAR"

"THE SOUTH HAS NOT MY SYMPATHIES"

While serving as Chancellor of the Exchequer, William E. Gladstone made a speech at Newcastle which created a furor in the press of the world and brought forth a sharp rebuke from Lord Russell.

From the speech at Newcastle, October 7, 1862:

> We know quite well that the people of the North-
> ern States have not yet drunk of the cup—they are
> still trying to hold it far from their lips—which all
> the rest of the world see they nevertheless must drink
> of. We may have our own opinions about slavery; we
> may be for or against the South; but there is no doubt
> that Jefferson Davis and other leaders of the South
> have made an army; they are making, it appears, a
> navy; and they have made what is more than either,
> they have made a nation.

Lord John Russell commented:

> You must allow me to say that I think you went
> beyond the latitude which all speakers must be al-
> lowed when you say that Jefferson Davis had made a
> nation. Recognition would seem to follow, and for
> that step I think the Cabinet is not prepared. . . .

*Gladstone to the Duchess of Sutherland, November
7, 1862:*

> A friendly correspondent writes to say he is sorry
> the South has my sympathies. But the South has not
> my sympathies, except in the sense in which the North
> has them also. I wish them both cordially well, which
> I believe is more than most Englishmen can at present
> say with truth. In both I see the elements of future
> power and good; in both I see also the elements of
> danger and mischief.

John Morley, THE LIFE OF WILLIAM EWART GLADSTONE

A VILE SPEECH AT NEWCASTLE

Shocked and angered by Gladstone's speech at Newcastle in which he acknowledged the South as a "nation," John Bright hastened to write his friend Charles Sumner three days later expressing his opinion of Gladstone's reckless statements.

Llandudno, North Wales, October 10, 1862
Dear Mr. Sumner,

I was very glad to receive your last letter containing much interesting information on the cotton question. I sent it and the letters, or copies of letters it contained to Mr. Cobden. It is quite clear that your Government was right in not sending an expedition to Texas, when it was a question whether it could keep a footing in Virginia.

I write to you from a feeling of anxiety. You will see what is being said here by public men who speak on your question, and most of all, and worst of all, by your old acquaintance and friend, Mr. Gladstone. He has made a vile speech at Newcastle, full of insulting pity for the North, and of praise and support for the South. He is unstable as water in some things.

He is for union and freedom in Italy, and for dis-union and bondage in America. A handful of Italians in prison in Naples, without formal trial, shocked his soul so much that he wrote a pamphlet, and has made many speeches upon it; but he has no word of sympathy or of hope for the four millions of the bondsmen of the South! I have known for months past that he talked of an European remonstrance, or mediation, or recognition, or some mischief of that kind, but I did not expect that he would step out openly as the defender and eulogist of Jeff. Davis and his fellow conspirators against God and man. He has spoken, as you will see by the time you receive this, and what he has said will encourage the friends of the South here to encreased exertions to promote something hostile to your Government and people. Palmerston and Russell, I fear, will not need much pressure to induce them to do anything they dare do on behalf of the permanent disruption of your Union.

Now, if I may trouble you again, I want you to write fully and frankly to me, that I may know what is possible and what is likely. If the "proclamation" means anything it means that you will preserve the Union, even tho' it involve a social revolution in the South and the transformation of four millions of slaves into as many laborers and peasants. If you destroy the armed force of the South still you will have a population deeply exasperated and disloyal, and government in their States must be difficult if not impossible. If the black nation can be made a population for the Union, then to hold the South may not be impossible; but without them, I see immeasurable difficulties in your path. Is the North prepared for all the hazards and for all the confusion which for a time such a course may render inevitable; and will the

Government be thoroughly supported by all the free States in such a policy? I conclude from the fact that the New York *Herald* has not dared to condemn the proclamation, that it meets with the support of your people. If the border States should not take fright at it, it seems to me calculated to be a powerful lever in future operations against the revolt. On these points we have, as yet, scarcely received any information, and I look for further tidings with great anxiety.

. . . I want you to tell me, if you can, what I may hope for, and what I may believe, that I may have my faith corrected or strengthened. Will the North persist? Will it grapple with the slavery devil and strangle it? May I believe that your country will be held together?

I begin to believe that another crop of cotton from slave labor will never again be grown on your Northern continent. Terribly as this would make me and mine and multitudes here to suffer, I cannot wish it otherwise. . . .

PROCEEDINGS OF THE MASSACHUSETTS HISTORICAL SOCIETY

AN EVALUATION OF LINCOLN

In the course of compiling a second edition of the works of Marx and Engels, three Russian historians discovered several unsigned letters from Karl Marx published in the Vienna

Presse, the newspaper for which he was a correspondent during the Civil War. The material which follows has been translated into English for the first time. The original appeared in *Die Presse,* October 12, 1862.

Lincoln is a figure *sui generis* in the annals of history. No pathos, no idealistic flights of eloquence, no posing, no wrapping himself in the toga of history. He always gives the most significant of his acts the most commonplace form. Where another man, acting for the sake of so many "square feet of land" declaims about "the struggle for an idea," Lincoln, even when he is acting for the sake of an idea, speaks only in terms of "square feet of land."

Indecisively, against his will, he reluctantly performs the *bravura aria* of his role as though asking pardon for the fact that circumstances are forcing him to "play the hero." The most formidable decrees which he hurls against the enemy and which will never lose their historic significance, resemble—as the author intends them to—ordinary summonses sent by one lawyer to another on the opposing side. . . . And this is the character the recent Proclamation bears—the most important document of American history since the founding of the Union, a document that breaks away from the old American Constitution —Lincoln's manifesto on the abolition of slavery. . . .

In the history of the United States and in the history of humanity, Lincoln occupies a place beside Washington! Truly in our day, when every little happening on this side of the Atlantic assumes an air of melodramatic portent, is there no meaning in the fact that everything of significance taking shape in the New World makes its appearance in such everyday form?

Lincoln was not born of a people's revolution. The ordinary play of the electoral system . . . bore him to its summit—a plebeian, who made his way from railsplitter to representative in Illinois, a man without intellectual brilliance, without special strength of character, not exceptionally impressive—an ordinary man of good will. Never yet has the New World scored a greater victory than in this instance, through its demonstration that, thanks to its political and social organization, ordinary people of good will can carry out tasks which the Old World would have to have a hero to accomplish!

In his day, Hegel remarked that in reality, comedy is above tragedy, the humor of the mind above its pathos. If Lincoln does not possess the gift of the pathos of historic action, he does as an ordinary man, coming from the people, possess the gift of the humor of that action. At what moment has Lincoln promulgated his Proclamation on the abolition of slavery in the territories of the Confederacy, to take effect on January 1, 1863? At that very moment when the Confederacy is adopting decisions, in the role of an independent state, at its congress in Richmond, on "peaceful negotiations." At that very moment, when the slave-owners of the border states believed that with the incursion of Southerners into Kentucky the "peculiar institution" would have been made as invincible as their invincible control over their countryman—the President in Washington, Abraham Lincoln.

Karl Marx, "ON THE CIVIL WAR AND LINCOLN"

THE "TIMES" ON THE
EMANCIPATION PROCLAMATION

London, October 14, 1862—The Emancipation Proclamation is an incitement to assassination. In truth, it
is nothing else, and can mean nothing else. . . .

London, October 21, 1862—Is the name of Lincoln
ultimately to be classed in the catalogue of monsters,
wholesale assassins and butchers of their kind? . . .
When blood begins to flow and shrieks come piercing
through the darkness, Mr. Lincoln will wait until the
rising flames tell that all is consummated, and then
he will rub his hands and think that revenge is
sweet. . . .

THE TIMES

A RUSSIAN DIPLOMAT REPORTS

Baron de Stoeckl, Russian Ambassador in Washington, to Prince Gortchakov, Minister for Foreign Affairs at
St. Petersburg:

I regret that no Russian naval officer was present to study the battle [*Merrimac* and *Monitor*]. It marks an epoch in naval history because it is the first serious engagement between armor-plated vessels. The battle shows beyond a doubt the superiority of armor-plated ships over wooden ones. These floating batteries have given new impetus to the American inventive genius.

Albert Woldman, LINCOLN AND THE RUSSIANS

TWO RACES ENCLOSED IN A SINGLE ARENA

Some of the literary giants of nineteenth-century Russia were regular but frequently anonymous contributors to periodicals which dared to publish controversial political and social ideas. One such publication was *Vremya* (*Time*), a magazine whose contents are considered by scholars to be largely the work of Feodor Dostoevsky. *Vremya's* title page bore the name of Mikhail Dostoevsky (Feodor's brother) as editor, since Feodor had but shortly returned from Siberian exile when the magazine was launched and he was still under police surveillance. Conceived primarily as an organ in which Feodor Dostoevsky could publish installments of his work in progress, it also served as a medium in which he could air his literary feuds and political views. A regular feature of *Vremya* was a section devoted to discussions of foreign affairs called "Contemporary Review." The following extracts are from articles which appeared in *Vremya* in 1861 and 1862, and are attributed to Feodor Dostoevsky by Russian scholars.

The events which are now taking place and those which have already taken place in America are opening up a new and perhaps final phase in the conflict over slavery and are of tremendous importance. Outstanding developments in the contemporary history of the Old World take second place when compared with the struggle that must precede the final reconciliation of white with black on American soil. Over there, two races—one might even say two humanities—are enclosed in a single arena in order to decide—by peaceful means or gun in hand—the greatest world problem.

One side is made up of planters who own the land, scions of the conquerors vaunting their intellect, will and wealth—men born of that noble white race which, by force of arms, through trade and industry, is gradually taking control of the entire world. The other side is made up of poverty-stricken slaves delivered up defenceless into the power of their masters, owning no property of any kind, neither the fields they plow nor the clothes they wear; people who are branded as inferior by the color of their skin; people subject to the lash, the rope and even fire by the arbitrary will of their masters, totally unrestrained. . . . The slave is a thing and not a human being. . . . The law specifies that the slave does not possess a soul. . . .

From Vremya, *December, 1862:*

The free forces lost 17,000 to 20,000 men—more, in actual fact, since these are the figures given by the commanders themselves. But the word "lost" is not the one to use here; it softens unjustifiably the utter horror of what is going on, turning the slaughter of 20,000 strong and healthy potentially useful men into something similar to the loss of a pair of gloves or the loss of 20,000 rubles. The insane wars of the First Empire left Europe with the bloody habit of viewing the loss of thousands and tens of thousands of people with indifference; but the time has come for mankind to reject this vicious custom. Twenty thousand men organized in a single line, standing shoulder to shoulder, take up some thirteen and a half versts. If each one of them were to be buried in an individual grave, in the normal manner usual for Christian people, they would occupy about 7,000 sagenes in a graveyard.

But even if this is nothing, if such colossal figures are nothing at all to us, then the loss can be assessed in terms of cash. Under the system of labor prevailing in the United States, each individual in sound health who is employed can easily earn his living and add 200 rubles over and above this annually to the national wealth. Through the destruction of 20,000 poor toilers, President Lincoln has reduced the national wealth by four million rubles annually. With interest at 4 per cent, this comes to a total of 100 million rubles. It is obvious that it would have been incomparably more profitable to have taken 100 million rubles worth of gold and, transporting it to the middle of the Atlantic, to have cast it 2,000 fathoms down into the water's depths. In addition to being very much more moral, it would also have been more profitable, since several millions had been wasted on the maintenance of those slain, as well as in the manufacture of their arms. . . .

The French government has proposed to the Russian and English governments that negotiations be entered into with the Washington Cabinet, and the request made for conclusion of an armistice between the warring sides which, thereafter, would in fact lead to peace. This proposal, however, has not been accepted. It is true that no one should intervene in the internal affairs of another state if it has no desire for this itself. But in the present situation this is highly regrettable. Blood is flowing, the slaves remain slaves, trade is at a standstill. Tens of thousands of families are without bread; the government is rapidly approaching bankruptcy; and now a new loan of 900 million rubles has been announced. . . .

Lincoln's decree, which he ought to have begun with if he had decided on extreme measures—freeing the slaves belonging to all those joining the rebellion —will lead to still greater bloodshed, to unheard-of savagery. The slaveholders are enraged in the extreme; and should they observe even the feeblest impulse in their slaves in the direction of implementing the expressed will of the President at Washington, will resort to the most ferocious measures to bring their slaves to heel. And up to the present time they have acted without ceremony. On the mere suspicion alone that certain whites in the slave states sympathized with the North and were assembling in order to carry out a harmless demonstration in favor of the North, they hanged scores of those suspected, *without trial* [italics in original], on hearsay alone. So you can imagine what they will do to the slaves who decide to put their trust in President Lincoln and think of themselves as free.

To all appearances, the war is being fought on account of slavery. . . . It would be a highly consoling thought for mankind that even if some tens of thousands perish their death would aid in the liberation of millions. Unfortunately, this is not so. The President's latest message blights this hope. President Lincoln declares that if the seceded states desire to come back into the Union, their "peculiar institution" shall remain theirs forever. It is in the name of this that softness toward slavery is called for. Words to this effect do not appear openly in the message; nothing is said about retaining slavery, but it is proposed that the slaves be redeemed by the Federal government in those states which shall themselves decide to abolish slavery by the year 1900. . . . It must be admitted that Mr. Lincoln is an extremely moderate abolitionist if he awaits nothing beyond this from the twentieth century. . . .

[*Attributed to Feodor Dostoevsky*], VREMYA

LETTER FROM THE
WORKING MEN OF MANCHESTER
TO PRESIDENT LINCOLN

Although the cotton mills of Manchester were shut down because of the cotton shortage, the unemployed workers of that city gathered at a mass meeting and drew up a letter to President Lincoln, conveying their admiration and support for the course he had followed in issuing the Emancipation Proclamation.

December 31, 1862

To His Excellency, Abraham Lincoln, President of the United States of America:

As citizens of Manchester, assembled at the Free Trade Hall, we beg to express our fraternal sentiments towards you and your country. We rejoice in your greatness as an outgrowth of England, whose blood and language you share, whose orderly and legal freedom you have applied to new circumstances, over a region immeasurably greater than our own. We honor your Free States, as a singularly happy abode for the working millions where industry is honored. One thing alone has, in the past, lessened our sympathy with your country and our confidence in it—we mean the ascendency of politicians who not merely maintained Negro slavery, but desired to extend and root it more firmly.

Since we have discerned, however, that the victory of the free North, in the war which has so sorely distressed us as well as afflicted you, will strike off the fetters of the slave, you have attracted our warm and earnest sympathy. We joyfully honor you, as the President, and the Congress with you, for many decisive steps toward practically exemplifying your belief in the words of your great founders: "All men are created free and equal." You have procured the liberation of the slaves in the district around Washington, and thereby made the centre of your Federation visibly free. You have enforced the laws against the slave-trade, and kept up your fleet against it, even while every ship was wanted for service in your terrible war. You have nobly decided to receive ambassadors from the Negro republics of Hayti and Liberia, thus forever renouncing that unworthy prejudice which refuses the rights of humanity to men and women on account of their color. In order more effectually to stop the slave-trade, you have made with our Queen a treaty, which your Senate has ratified, for the right of mutual search. Your Congress has decreed freedom as the law forever in the vast unoccupied or half unsettled Territories which are directly subject to its legislative power. It has offered pecuniary aid to all States which will enact emancipation locally, and has forbidden your Generals to restore fugitive slaves who seek their protection. You have entreated the slave-masters to accept these moderate offers; and after long and patient waiting, you, as Commander-in-Chief of the Army, have appointed to-morrow, the first of January, 1863, as the day of unconditional freedom for the slaves of the rebel States.

Heartily do we congratulate you and your country on this humane and righteous course. We assume that you cannot now stop short of a complete uprooting of slavery. It would not become us to dictate any details, but there are broad principles of humanity which must guide you. If complete emancipation in some States be deferred, though only to a predetermined day, still in the interval, human beings should not be counted chattels. Women must have the rights of chastity and maternity, men the rights of husbands, masters the liberty of manumission. Justice demands for the black, no less than for the white, the protection of law—that his voice be heard in your courts. Nor must any such abomination be tolerated as slave-breeding States, and a slave market —if you are to earn the high reward of all your sacrifices, in the approval of the universal brotherhood and of the Divine Father. It is for your free country to decide whether any thing but immediate and total emancipation can secure the most indispensable rights of humanity against the inveterate wickedness of local laws and local executives.

We implore you, for your own honor and welfare, not to faint in your providential mission. While your enthusiasm is aflame, and the tide of events runs high, let the work be finished effectually. Leave no root of bitterness to spring up and work fresh misery to your children. It is a mighty task, indeed, to reorganize the industry not only of four millions of the colored race, but of five millions of whites. Nevertheless, the vast progress you have made in the short space of twenty months fills us with hope that every stain on

200

your freedom will shortly be removed, and that the erasure of that foul blot upon civilization and Christianity—chattel slavery—during your Presidency will cause the name of Abraham Lincoln to be honored and revered by posterity. We are certain that such a glorious consummation will cement Great Britain to the United States in close and enduring regards. Our interests, moreover, are identified with yours. We are truly one people, though locally separate. And if you have any ill-wishers here, be assured they are chiefly those who oppose liberty at home, and that they will be powerless to stir up quarrels between us, from the very day in which your country becomes, undeniably and without exception, the home of the free.

Accept our high admiration of your firmness in upholding the proclamation of freedom.

MANCHESTER GUARDIAN

"I WOULD HAVE A 'TE DEUM' NOT A 'MISERERE' SUNG"

Letter from Fredrika Bremer to Marcus and Rebecca Springs:

Stockholm 10th Jan. 1863

Dearest friends Marcus and Rebecca!

Yesterday night I read by my evening lamp in our papers a report from New York of the terrible battle at

Fred[e]ri[c]ksburg. . . . It made my night restless, but now as the morning of a dim and dark winter day dawns over me and tears dim my eyes while writing to you I feel something bright and great in my heart a swelling of pride and joy. Why so? Dear friends, there is something in war greater than victory and success, it is the unflinching, heroic sacrifice of life for the cause of right and duty it is the brave resolute death on the battle field. The bloody affair . . . is to my eyes one of the noblest deeds of your Armies, and as I believe certainly one which will more than many victories win the admiration of Europe to your spirit and its sympat[h]ies to your cause. I would to its commemoration have in your cities a "Te Deum" not a "Miserere" sung. . . .

So far had I written when the postman brought me an American paper with Marcus' dear handwriting on it. It was the Christian examiner and it gave me joy to see by it how Unitarians in England begin to feel for your cause, and also to see how generously in the midst of the heavy taxes for war you at the same time are doing for the unfortunate operatives in England thrown out of work by this war! Even the Northern Iron working provinces of my land are suffering from it. My faith is firm in its final issue. . . .

Signe A. Rooth, SEERESS OF THE NORTHLAND

EDITORIAL FROM THE ST. PETERS-BURG "VEDOMOSTI" ON THE EMANCIPATION PROCLAMATION

January, 1863—The accusations to which Mr. Lincoln is subjected may be reduced to two principal heads. First of all, they assert that his proclamation is called forth not by principle, but by interest; not from conviction, but from necessity; that he promulgated it only when he had lost every hope of seeing the southern States voluntarily returned to the Union; that he retains slavery where he might have abolished it, and abolished it only where it is out of his power to do so; that its abolition is meant (according to the London *Times*) as a punishment for rebellion, and its preservation as a reward for loyalty to the Union. In these accusations, the more personal question is curiously mixed up with the real substance of the act. It is of no great importance for us to know by what successive convictions Mr. Lincoln was guided to its accomplishment. The act of emancipation itself is the only important thing, viewed with reference to the reasons which finally led to its promulgation. A pure, benevolent deed may spring from an impure impulse, and the action called forth by necessity may be at the same time perfectly just.

What would be said of the historian who should condemn the Magna Charta, because it was granted by the miserable King John?

Mr. Lincoln never was an abolitionist, and it is true that during the first year of his government his policy was by no means favorable to immediate emancipation. But among his advisers and friends, upon whom the *Times* almost invokes damnation, many have been for years devoted to the cause of emancipation, and to them, certainly, the proclamation of January 1 has a deeper significance than a mere measure of public safety. They co-operated in preparing the proclamation, and therefore it cannot be considered as only the result of a calculation. For the benefit as well as for the honor of the Federal government, it would have been better if the war against the South had taken the character of a war against slavery at its very outset, but the emancipationists were yet too weak, the desire to preserve the Union and the prejudice against the Negro too strong. Time and circumstances have changed the state of the case, and the services of Mr. Lincoln consist in his having ventured to make use of the opportunity. We do not see anything especially heroic in the fact, but still less can we call it shameful. We may perhaps be asked, Why has not Mr. Lincoln liberated the slaves in the States remaining loyal to the Union? Here we find, in the arguments of the *Times* and other pro-slavery papers, a very singular contradiction. They incessantly repeat that the proclamation of January 1 is a clearly unjust and treacherous violation of the Constitution, and at the same time they blame Mr. Lincoln for not having committed a violation ten times more glaring and unjust. The Constitution of the United States does not allow the central power to interfere in the local institutions of the separate States, and slavery is one of these institutions. The Southern States having seceded from the Union, having declared the Constitution as invalid for them, have naturally lost all the rights which it guaranteed to them. Therefore, the abolition of slavery in these States may be proclaimed without violating the Constitution. But the border States which remained loyal to the Union, are still under its protection. In reference to them, the President and Congress have only such rights as the central power possesses in ordinary times of peace. The Federal government may and should use every possible means to induce them, voluntarily, to adopt emancipation, but so long as the Constitution remains unchanged, it has no right to force them. The President has manifested his determination to use every means in his power to promote the voluntary abolition of slavery in the border States; to demand of him more than this would be unjust, as the *Times* well understands. It is to be hoped that the same force of circumstances which gave rise to the proclamation, will lead the border States to emancipation; and this, in our opinion, is the best result of Mr. Lincoln's policy.

Let us now refer to the other accusation. . . . Mr. Lincoln is charged with inciting the slaves to rebellion against their masters, by his proclamation. Then follows a series of eloquent phrases about innocent wives and children, torrents of blood, each drop of which will fall on Mr. Lincoln's head. . . . Here, again, we notice a few contradictions and inconsistencies. At one time, the proclamation is represented as a dead letter not worth the pen with which it was signed; but now it is the all-powerful word, whose utterance shall bring forth thunders and convulsions. But we leave these contradictions, which testify only to the blind partisanship of the friends of the South.

DIPLOMATIC CORRESPONDENCE, 1864

ITALIAN LIBERALS HAIL THE EMANCIPATION PROCLAMATION

The first signer of this address to President Lincoln was Garibaldi.

If in the midst of your Titanic battles, our voice can yet reach you, let us, O Lincoln, free sons of Columbus, send you a word of good wishes and of admiration for the great work that you have begun. Heir of the aspirations of Christ and of John Brown, you will pass to posterity with the name of the Emancipator; more enviable than any crown or any human treasure. . . .

Let free men religiously keep sacred the day of the fall of slavery . . . prosperity to you, Abraham Lincoln, pilot of liberty; hail to all you who for two years have fought and died around her regenerating banner; weal to you, redeemed sons of Ham—the free men of Italy kiss the glorious marks of your chains.

Albert Woldman, LINCOLN AND THE RUSSIANS

THE "TIMES" VERSUS THE BIBLE

To support its violent attacks on the Emancipation Proclamation, the London *Times* on January 6, 1863, gave its interpretation of the New Testament.

In that Bible which is always appealed to by abolitionist fanatics, there is not one single text that can be perverted to prove that Slavery is unlawful. . . . Slavery is indeed contrary to the spirit of the New Testament, but so also are sumptuous fare, purple and fine linen, wealth, ecclesiastical titles, unmarried clergy, good clerical income and many other things.

EMANCIPATION IS BUT

A PRETEXT

Alphonse de Lamartine, member of the French Academy, poet, novelist and statesman, achieved immediate

success with his first publication, a
collection of poems. After a brief and
disillusioning political career he devoted himself to writing.

As for this question of slavery, noble pretext of their
present war, what the cause means over there is made
quite clear by a statement of their President. Mr.
Lincoln proclaimed in Congress that nobody among
the Northerners would wish to acknowledge a Negro
as his brother, or as a relation, and that he himself
shared that glorious prejudice; and that if, as President, he had gone to war for this abject race, as an
American he despised it and repudiated it like all his
compatriots. So, in the North, the Negroes are enduring and will continue to endure the law of contempt, their poverty will set them apart from the
rest of the population, their race will slowly die out
from starvation, and all of this will be taking place
in the very federation which claims to be waging
war for the liberty and the equality of the Negro
race. As for equality, you have only to question the
European travelers who have lived in Northern
states, supposedly liberators of the Negro race, to be
enlightened on the subject. To be treated everywhere
as lepers, is that equality? To bring shame on a family
simply by contracting an alliance with some member
of it, is that equality? To be ejected from theatres
and public places, is that equality? To be consigned
to special cars on the railways, as we would do in
France in the case of unclean animals, is that equality?

All of this should be sufficient to show that the
emancipation of the Negro race is but a pretext in
this war against the South, and that the true motive

is passionate jealousy of the South, whose black capital, whose cotton, whose powerful navy and flourishing trade excites the murderous envy of this people forever determined to reduce everything to its own level. But the six million Negroes in the South are not fooled. They haven't hesitated one second between a state of bondage in which they are fed and protected by their masters, and the ferocious irresponsibility of their advocates in the North who urge them to rebel. They prefer the compulsory work, the providential care of their Southern exploiters to the criminal irresponsibility of the North. To be free and to die of hunger appeals to them very little. They prefer the humiliation of legal bondage to the neglect of the alleged philanthropists of the North. And if they must suffer torments, they prefer, quite rightly, those of slavery, which at least provides them with a roof over their heads and food and wages, to those of contempt and death in the North.

For a long time I have been an ardent promoter of emancipation of the Negroes . . . and indemnity for their proprietors. You must understand that the slave is a bad type of property, but he is nevertheless a legal type of property, and the state has guaranteed this property in exactly the same way it has any other; you cannot expropriate without offering compensation to the owner and without giving him the means to pay a wage to the freed slave for the work he will not freely furnish.

This is what the very rich Americans of the Northern states should have said to the Southerners: "Emancipate your slaves, gradually, prudently and together we will raise the sum that will be necessary to pay for free labor in the dispossessed states."

Alphonse de Lamartine, COURS FAMILIER DE LITTÉRATURE

NAPOLEON III SPEAKS FRANKLY

In a speech to the Legislature on January 12, 1863, the French Emperor discussed the effect of the American war on the French economy:

The indirect revenues show a continual increase, from the simple fact of the general increase of prosperity, and the condition of the Empire would be flourishing if the American war had not dried up one of the most fruitful sources of our industry. The forced stagnation of labor has caused in many districts an amount of destitution which deserves all our solicitude, and a grant will be asked from you for the support of those who with resignation submit to the effects of a misfortune which it is not in our power to put a stop to. Nevertheless, I have made the attempt to send beyond the Atlantic advices inspired by a sincere sympathy; but, the great maritime powers not having thought it advisable as yet to act in concert with me, I have been obliged to postpone to a more suitable opportunity the offer of mediation, the object of which was to stop the effusion of blood and to prevent the exhaustion of a country, the future of which cannot be looked upon with indifference. . . .

APPLETON'S ANNUAL ENCYCLOPEDIA, 1863

The following month Napoleon informed his Councilors:

If the North is victorious, I shall be happy; if the
South is victorious, I shall be enchanted!

John Bigelow, RETROSPECTIONS OF AN ACTIVE LIFE

FRANCE SUFFERS FROM THE
BLOCKADE

At the very gates of Paris one hundred and thirty
thousand people were out of work. . . . In England
the worst is over. Here, the worst is not yet discovered. . . . Unfortunate people crept from door to door
in the country asking for bread and shelter. Around
Rouen, twenty-six thousand people were estimated
to be in utter destitution.

REVUE DES DEUX MONDES

Where is progress in France? Cotton weavers of
Rouen now eat grass, mothers register their daughters as prostitutes!"

Jules and Edmond de Goncourt, MEMOIRS DE LA VIE LITTERAIRE

FRENCH COTTON WORKERS
OPPOSE INTERVENTION

Eugène Forcade, in his February 1, 1863, column, "Chronique de la Quinzaine," discusses the attitude of the factory workers in Normandy.

These men [cotton workers of Rouen] who have been suffering so terribly because of the lack of raw material in the cotton mills nevertheless understand that the present crisis was brought about by a superior cause, against which the human will is powerless. But what is even more remarkable is that they also understand that this crisis does not give anybody the right to intervene in the American conflict. . . . What a strange contrast! Our government seems sincerely concerned with the situation of our cotton workers and shows great impatience with the Americans and their Civil War. England and Russia having firmly refused to participate in any kind of joint peace intervention, our government, alone this time, has suggested to the Washington government that peace overtures be made to the Secessionists, without suspending hostilities. Such a step would only favor the South and displease the North. It would give new hopes to the Southerners. Here then is this strange contrast: While our government shows definite partiality for the Southern cause, in the hope of obtaining the raw material for our cotton workers, these same workers take a very different view of the matter. If they were asked the following question: "Which do you prefer—victory for the South, with the reappearance of cotton on our markets and the continuation of slavery, or the emancipation of the whole of the Negro race with unemployment and hunger persisting among you as a result?"—we are quite certain that their answer would be: "Without a moment's hesitation, we would rather go on suffering poverty and hunger than see four million human beings continue to live in bondage."

Eugène Forcade, "CHRONIQUE DE LA QUINZAINE"

"OUR COUNTRY ACCEPTS
WITH GRATITUDE"

The South, in an attempt to break England's neutrality and gain her support, withheld and burned its cotton, thus forcing a complete shutdown in the Lancashire cotton mills. "The agony of Lancashire," said the London *Times* "is every day becoming more acute, and before the winter is ended the sufferings of the people will prove the greatest national trial that we have had since the Irish famine." "I see that someone in the States has proposed to send something to our aid," John Bright wrote to Charles Sumner in December, 1862. "If a few cargoes of flour could come, say, 50,000 barrels, as a gift from persons in your Northern States to the Lancashire working men, it would have a prodigious effect in your favor here. Our working class is with you, and against the South, but such a token of your good will would cover with confusion all who talk against you."

In the winter of 1862–1863 an International Relief Committee was set up in New York to raise funds and supplies for the suffering mill hands. Numerous meetings were held in the cotton-manufacturing districts to express the gratitude of the destitute operatives. The following is a resolution of thanks addressed to the commander of the relief ship *George Griswold.*

February, 1863

Sir:

Sixteen years ago when our countrymen in Ireland were suffering the horrors of famine, your nation—then united and prosperous—sent across the Atlantic offerings of grain and provisions to alleviate their great distress. To-day, with your energies taxed to the utmost by the gigantic struggle through which you are passing, you have not ceased to be mindful of the misery which this sad conflict is inflicting on fully half a million of our industrious workers; and you have a second time generously contributed to help those among us, who, through no fault of their own, are reduced to a state of compulsory idleness and destitution.

May we not hope that the trial through which you and we are passing, will be the precursor of great social ameliorations; and that out of the darkest hour of a nation's existence—that of bloodshed between members of the same family—there may arise for you some signal national deliverance, the benefits of which are to stretch beyond yourselves, to the gain of our common humanity.

Our country accepts with gratitude the noble gift. We welcome to our port the bearers of this brotherly bounty—freely given—freely stowed—and freely freighted across the seas by a commander who has given his service to this benevolent work. Our government and the local authorities have shown their appreciation of the act, by removing every impost on the free admission of the ship and her cargo. . . .

Addressing you on behalf of a community among whom, it is well known, great differences of opinion prevail as to the causes and objects of the contest now unhappily raging among you, it would be evidently unbecoming in us to put forward any statement that would create dissension and mar the general harmony of the occasion; but we think we are warranted in saying that men of all shades of opinion would rejoice to see this war terminated in any way that would not be inconsistent with your honor as a people, and with the great and responsible position which you occupy among the nations. We trust that nothing will arise to interrupt, for a moment, the friendly relations which have hitherto subsisted between us; and that no harsh judgments, or misrepresentations of feelings and motives, on either side, will lead us to forget that we are kinsmen sprung from a common stock, united by the bond of a common language, and fellow-laborers in the common cause of progress.

May the two great branches of the Anglo-Saxon family always be found generous rivals in the arts of peace, and in efforts to ameliorate the condition of mankind! And, at no distant period, may the sword be sheathed throughout your land, and the sound of strife be exchanged for the conquests of industry.

Signed on behalf of the Liverpool Chamber of Commerce.

R. A. Macfie, President.

"REPORT OF THE AMERICAN INTERNATIONAL RELIEF COMMITTEE"

SONG OF THE UNEMPLOYED COTTON WORKERS

The unexpected—and unwanted—windfall of leisure time among the unemployed operatives in the Lancashire districts was put to constructive use. Improvised schoolrooms were set up and the rudiments of education were made available for the first time for most of these people. The following verse, expressing their thanks for gifts of flour and other relief from America, originated among these temporary "students."

Our mules and looms have now ceased work, the Yankees are the cause
But we will let them fight it out and stand by English laws
No recognizing shall take place, until the war is o'er:
Our wants are now attended to, we cannot ask for more.

E. D. *Adams,* GREAT BRITAIN AND THE AMERICAN CIVIL WAR

LETTER FROM JOHN RUSKIN
TO CHARLES ELIOT NORTON

10th February, 1863
Mornex, Haute Savoie

It is no use talking about your war. There is a religious phrensy on such of you as are good for anything, just as wild, foolish and fearful as St. Dominic's and as obstinate as de Montfort's. Mahomet's was mild, Christian-like, rational in comparison. I have not, however, seen a single word, spoken or written by any American since the war began, which would justify me in assuming that there was any such noble phrensy in the matter, but as Lowell and you are in it, I am obliged to own to nobility and only wish I could put you both in straight waistcoats.

The miserablest idiocy of the whole thing has been your mixing up in a fight for dominion (the most insolent and tyrannical, and the worst conducted in all history) with a *soi-disant* fight for liberty. If you want the slaves to be free, let their masters go free first, in God's name. If they don't like to be governed by you, let them govern themselves. *Then* treating them as a stranger State, if you like to say, "You shall let that black fellow go or"—etc., as a brave boy would fight another for a bag at Eton—do so; but you know perfectly well no fight could be got up on these terms; and that this fight is partly for money, partly for vanity, partly (as these wretched Irish whom you have inveigled into it show) for wild anarchy and the Devil's crown everywhere. As for your precious Proclamation . . . if I had it here— there's a fine north wind blowing and I would give it to the first boy I met to fly it at his kite's tail.

As soon as I get a house, I'll ask you to send me something American—a slave, perhaps. I've a great notion of a black boy in a green jacket and purple cap—in Paul Veronese's manner. . . .

Cook and Wedderburn, eds., LETTERS OF JOHN RUSKIN

APPEAL FROM THE
PROTESTANT PASTORS OF FRANCE

Addressed to the pastors and ministers of all evangelical denominations in Great Britain, this appeal originally carried 600 signatures and by the end of March, 1863, the number had increased to 789.

Paris, February 12, 1863

Brothers Honored and Beloved in The Lord: . . .

The civilized world has contemplated nothing more revolting than a confederation, in great part Protestant, organizing itself and claiming independence, with the openly avowed intention of maintaining and propagating slavery; and laying as the corner-stone of its constitution the system of slavery actually in existence in the southern States, and which may be defined to be the right to treat men as cattle, and give impunity to adultery and homicide. Let us lay aside all considerations of policy. Is there a Christian who does not shudder when he hears the chief of this confederation reply to a decree of emancipation by a sort of menace of extermination? The triumph of such a cause would throw back for a century that of Christian civilization and of humanity; would cause angels in heaven to weep, and would rejoice the demons in hell. . . . Pastors, ministers of all evangelical denominations of England, of Scotland, of Ireland . . . place yourselves at our head, and stir up altogether a great and peaceful demonstration of sympathy for the black race, so long enchained and abased by Christian nations.

Discourage thus the partisans of slavery, fortify and strengthen those who would abolish it, whilst preparing them to accept our counsels. What may we not hope, if throughout Great Britain the voice of all the ministers of the Crucified, and in France our voice echoing theirs, should pray and petition that soon there may not be in the United States a single black man who is not free, a single black not upon equality with the white. . . .

DIPLOMATIC CORRESPONDENCE, 1864

EMANCIPATION PROCLAMATION STRENGTHENS ANTI-SLAVERY FEELING IN ENGLAND

Richard Cobden assures Charles Sumner that the Emancipation Proclamation has turned the tide of public opinion in England and ended the possibility of intervention.

Athenaeum Club, London, 13 Feby., 1863

Private

My dear Sumner.

If I have not written to you before it is not because I have been indifferent to what is passing in your midst. I may say sincerely that my thoughts have run almost as much on American as English politics. But I could do you no service, and shrunk from occupying your overtaxed attention even for a moment. My object in now writing is to speak of a matter which has a practical bearing on your affairs.

You know how much alarmed I was from the first lest our government should interpose in your affairs. This disposition of our ruling class, and the necessities of our cotton trade, pointed to some act of intervention and the indifference of the great mass of our population to your struggle, the object of which they did not foresee and understand, would have made intervention easy indeed popular if you had been a weaker naval power. This state of feeling existed up to the announcement of the President's emancipation Policy. From that moment our old anti-slavery feeling began to arouse itself, and it has been gathering strength ever since. The great rush of the public to all the public meetings called on the subject shows how wide and deep the sympathy for personal freedom still is in the hearts of our people.

I know nothing in my political experience so striking as a display of spontaneous public action as that of the vast gathering at Exeter Hall when without one attraction in the form of a popular orator the vast building, its minor rooms and passages and the streets adjoining were crowded with an enthusiastic audience. That meeting has had a powerful effect on our newspapers and politicians. It has closed the mouths of those who have been advocating the side of the South.

And I now write to assure you that any unfriendly act on the part of our government, no matter which of our aristocratic parties is in power, towards your cause is not to be apprehended. If an attempt were made by the government in any way to commit us to the South, a spirit would be instantly aroused which would drive our government from power. This I suppose will be known and felt by the Southern agents in Europe and if communicated to their government must I should think operate as a great discouragement to them. For I *know* that those agents have been incessantly urging in every quarter where they could hope to influence the French and English governments the absolute necessity of *recognition* as a means of putting an end to the war. Recognition of the South, by England, whilst it bases itself on Negro slavery, is an impossibility, unless indeed after the Federal government have recognized the Confederates as a nation.

So much for the influence which your emancipation policy has had on the public opinion of England. But judging from the tone of your press in America it does not seem to have gained the support of your masses. About this however I do not feel competent to offer an opinion. Nor, to confess the truth, do I feel much satisfaction in treating of your politics at all. There appears to me great mismanagement I had almost said incapacity in the management of your affairs, and you seem to be hastening towards financial and economical evils in a manner which fills me with apprehension for the future.

When I met Fremont in Paris two years ago just as you commenced this terrible war I remarked to him that the total abolition of slavery in your northern Continent was the only issue which could justify the war to the civilized world. Every symptom seems to point to this result. But at what a price is the Negro to be emancipated! I confess that if then I had been the arbiter of his fate I should have refused him freedom at the cost of so much white men's blood and women's tears. I do not however blame the North. The South fired the first shot, and on them righteously falls the malediction that "they who take the sword shall perish by the sword."

Believe me,
Yours very truly
R. Cobden

Edward L. Pierce,
LETTERS OF RICHARD COBDEN TO CHARLES SUMNER

LETTER FROM CHARLES DARWIN
TO ASA GRAY

Down, February 23 [1863].

I read Cairn's excellent Lecture, which shows so well how your quarrel arose from Slavery. It made me for a time wish honestly for the North; but I could never help, though I tried, all the time thinking how we should be bullied and forced into a war by you, when you were triumphant. But I do most truly think it dreadful that the South, with its accursed slavery, should triumph and spread the evil. I think if I had power, which, thank God, I have not, I would let you conquer the border States, and all west of the Mississippi, and then force you to acknowledge the cotton states. For do you not now begin to doubt whether you can conquer and hold them? . . .

The *Times* is getting more detestable (but that is too weak a word) than ever. My good wife wishes to give it up, but I tell her that is a pitch of heroism to which only a woman is equal. To give up the "Bloody Old *Times,*" as Cobbett used to call it, would be to give up meat, drink and air. Farewell, my dear Gray.

Yours most truly,
C. *Darwin.*

Francis Darwin, LIFE AND LETTERS OF CHARLES DARWIN

LETTER FROM JOHN BRIGHT
TO JOHN GREENLEAF WHITTIER

In a charming letter to a fellow
Quaker, John Bright acknowledges a
contribution of funds raised in America for the Lancashire unemployed.

February 27, 1863

Thy letter has given me much pleasure. The contribution enclosed in it, I have paid over to the Secretary of the Lancashire Relief Fund in Manchester.
Thy letter and the report of the meeting at Amesbury have been published in the Manchester "Examiner & Times," the most widely circulated paper in
the North of England. I am sure the kindness toward
our people indicated by the contributions has given
much pleasure in many quarters. . . . I have been a
warm admirer and a constant reader of thy poems for
many years, and I can imagine something of the deep
interest which the great conflict must excite in thee.
It seems as if a peaceable termination of the great
evil of slavery was impossible—the blindness, the
pride and the passion of men make it impossible.
War was and is the only way out of the desperate
difficulty of your country, and fearful as is the path,
it cannot be escaped. I only hope there may be

virtue enough in the North, notwithstanding the terrible working of the poison of slavery, to throw off the coils, and to permit of a renovated and restored nation. . . . With us we are witnessing a great change of opinion, or opinions hitherto silent are being expressed. In every town a great meeting is being held, to discuss the "American question" and the vote is almost everywhere unanimously in favor of the North. The rich and the titled may hate the republic, but the *people* do not.

My daughter sometimes sends thee a newspaper with a report of some speech of mine. She is as much an American in sympathy as I am, and she wishes me to say how much pleasure she has derived from all thy poems, and how much she hopes all thy noble words for freedom may soon bear fruit throughout your country. I await tidings from the States with anxiety—but I have faith in freedom and good. With many thanks for thy kind note and for the sympathy with our people manifested by the Amesbury contribution, believe me always,

Thy Sincere Friend,
John Bright.

Samuel T. Pickard,
LIFE AND LETTERS OF JOHN GREENLEAF WHITTIER

THE FINGER OF PROVIDENCE

Member of the Belgian Chamber of Representatives, Canon de Haerne was an eminent and popular Catholic theologian. He was also the founder and director of the *Spectator Belge*, a liberal intellectual periodical.

In the present state of American society, considering especially the moral abyss which prejudices have caused between the two races . . . what ought to be desired is to behold in those [Southern] States the numerous and beautiful schools, of which America is so justly proud, thrown open to men of color and especially to the children of slaves, who are at the present for the most part excluded therefrom; to see spring up in those States, in accordance with the liberty of instruction written in the constitutions of the States, a happy and fraternal emulation between the Catholics and Protestants in order that Americans might say with truth that nearly all their children are instructed, and that they have not to add this humiliating restriction: except the blacks and mulattoes who form a third of the population of the South. . . .

The American question . . . greatly interests the entire world, and especially Europe. The material interests of manufacturing countries and especially those of England are seriously mixed up in this question as far as the manufacture of cotton is concerned, on which the fate of about four million labourers depends, directly or indirectly in the latter country, and that of more than three million in the remainder of the civilised world, the United States included. America suffers more from the cotton crisis than Europe; the North suffers like England and the European continent from the dearth of the raw material. The South injures itself by its political fanaticism, result of despair, by destroying its cotton in order to compel the European powers and especially England to take an interest in its cause. But the South is not only doing itself a considerable momentary injury, an injury which certainly does not argue in favour of the civilisation of which it boasts; it also causes itself a great detriment for the future, giving to the production of cotton, owing to its high price a very great impulse in every country of the globe where the climate permits of its culture. This is what the English are endeavouring to effect with all the energy which characterizes them. If after the war, the agriculture of the cotton States returns to its former condition, which is not probable, the capital engaged in this cultivation in India, China, Egypt, Algiers, and elsewhere, will greatly increase the competition with America. . . .

Thus, no matter in what light we regard the American question, we are led to this conclusion, that the social commotion which agitates the Union will turn against slavery, and consequently against the intentions of the separatists. The most certain result of success for the South would be a continual intervention of Europe in the American affairs, which would forcibly lead to the suppression of slavery without indemnity. Who could help seeing in these grave events the finger of Providence, which brings about insensibly, but surely and by hidden means of which men ignore the import, the triumph of Christian civilisation and the teaching of the Gospel, not as some Protestants understand it, who often turn it to suit their prejudices, but as it has always been proclaimed and is still practised by the Catholic Church? Christian emancipation and the development of commerce have always gone hand in hand. . . .

The threat of the *Monitor*, like that of the French

navy, has been understood. A country which can bring forward in a few months 600,000 men, drilled after European fashion, and equip sea forces proportionate to this land army, evidently ranks as a great power, with which Europe will have to contend sooner or later. . . .

Instead of secretly combatting this new power, we should frankly accept it, since it exists and fortifies itself through the very opposition it expects to meet with from Europe. . . . Who knows if America, through its unceasingly increasing strength, is not destined to force the European powers to return to conservative traditions, now generally abandoned by them, through the danger of democratic ideas, which a war with the American States would not fail to strengthen in Europe? If the wars of the First Empire and that of the Crimea had the effect of propagating liberal ideas in Russia, as the war of American independence influenced the French Revolution of 1789, would not a conflict between America and certain countries of Europe produce the same effects in the latter? For this reason the giant, who stands on the other side of the Atlantic, and whose audacity augments the strength which he possesses by nature and youth, can no longer be despised. We must reckon with him and when he exerts himself towards civilisation, as in the question of the emancipation of slaves, we must second his efforts by regulating them by means of a wise co-operation as far as we are able. This is an idea which President Lincoln expressed when he said to the European powers: If you require cotton, aid us in bringing to reason the men who burn it hoping thereby to gain your assistance, and who thus plunge all commercial countries into a frightful crisis. An alliance with the North for the

229

sake of humanity and for a reciprocal interest . . .
would be the thing most to be desired in the present
state of affairs; but if we do not make haste, the
time may very possibly come when nothing can be
done either to bring about peace or the rational
abolition of slavery.

Canon de Haerne, THE AMERICAN QUESTION

PRIVILEGE CURSES
THE AMERICAN REPUBLIC

John Bright's famous speech to the
trade unions of London at St. James's
Hall, March, 1863:

Privilege thinks it has a great interest in this contest,
and every morning, with blatant voice, it comes into
your streets and curses the American Republic.
Privilege has beheld an afflicting spectacle for many
years past. It has beheld thirty millions of men,
happy and prosperous, without emperor, without
king, without the surroundings of a court, without
nobles, except such as are made by eminence in intellect and virtue, without State bishops and State
priests . . . without great armies and great navies,
without great debt and without great taxes. Privilege has shuddered at what might happen to old

Europe if this grand experiment should succeed. But you, the workers—you, striving after a better time—you struggling upwards towards the light, with slow and painful steps, you have no cause to look with jealousy upon a country which, amongst all the great nations of the globe, is that one where labour has met with the highest honour, and where it has reaped its greatest reward. Are you aware of the fact, that in fifteen years, which is but as yesterday when it is past, two and a half millions of your countrymen have found a home in the United States—that a population equal nearly, if not quite, to the population of this great city—itself equal to no mean kingdom—has emigrated from these shores? In the United States there has been, as you know, an open door for every man—and millions have entered into it, and have found rest.

Now, take the two sections of the country which are engaged in this fearful struggle. In the one labour is honoured more than elsewhere in the world; there, more than in any other country, men rise to competence and independence; a career is open; the pursuit of happiness is not hopelessly thwarted by the law. In the other section of that country, labour is not only not honoured, but it is degraded. The labourer is made a chattel. He is no more his own than the horse that drags a carriage through the next street; nor is his wife, nor is his child, nor is anything that is his, his own.

There may be men—rich men—in this city of London, who will buy in the slave-owners' loan, and who, for the chance of more gain than honest dealing will afford them, will help a conspiracy whose fundamental institution, whose cornerstone, is declared to be felony, and infamous by the statutes of their country.

I speak not to these men—I leave them to their conscience in that hour which comes to all of us, when conscience speaks and the soul is no longer deaf to her voice. I speak rather to you, the working men of London, the representatives, as you are here tonight, of the feelings and the interests of the millions who cannot hear my voice. I wish you to be true to yourselves. Dynasties may fall, aristocracies may perish, privilege will vanish into the dim past; but you, your children, and your children's children, will remain, and from you the English people will be continued to succeeding generations.

You wish the freedom of your country. You wish it for yourselves. You strive for it in many ways. Do not then give the hand of fellowship to the worst foes of freedom that the world has ever seen, and do not, I beseech you, bring down a curse upon your cause which no after penitence can ever lift from it. You will not do this. I have faith in you. Impartial history will tell that, when your statesmen were hostile or coldly neutral, when many of your rich men were corrupt, when your press—which ought to have instructed and defended—was mainly written to betray, the fate of a continent and of its vast population being in peril, you clung to freedom with an unfaltering trust that God in his infinite mercy will yet make it the heritage of all His children.

George Macaulay Trevelyan, LIFE OF JOHN BRIGHT

DISRAELI LOOKS INTO THE FUTURE

Benjamin Disraeli, brilliant British statesman and author, revitalized the Tory party after its split by Robert Peel and became the spokesman for the Tories when he was elected to Parliament in 1837. Disraeli was Chancellor of the Exchequer from 1858–59 and after continued opposition to the governments of Palmerston and Russell became Prime Minister in 1867. The following excerpt is from a speech in the House of Commons early in 1863.

I have always looked upon the struggle in America in the light of a great revolution. . . . Who ever may be young enough to live to witness the ultimate consequences of this Civil War, will see, whenever the waters have subsided, a different America from that which was known to our fathers and even from that of which this generation has had so much experience. It will be an America of armies, of diplomacy, of Rival States and manoeuvring Cabinets, of frequent turbulence and probably of frequent wars. . . .

W. F. Monypenny and George E. Buckle,
LIFE OF BENJAMIN DISRAELI, EARL OF BEACONSFIELD

SOUTHERN AID MOVEMENT IN ENGLAND

Financial support of the rebel cause became an organized movement in England, headed by Lord Wharncliffe and backed by some of the most powerful industrialists and reactionary members of Parliament. The most effective implementation of this aid was the establishment of the London and Confederate States Bank with a capitalization of two million pounds. On March 14, 1863, the following "preliminary prospectus" was issued announcing the reasons for such a move. Another facet of the Southern aid movement and the vast sums of money it could raise appears directly below the "prospectus." In this Lord Wharncliffe appeals to American Ambassador Adams for permission to send seventeen thousand pounds raised at a bazaar for the relief of Southern prisoners of war.

In organizing the proposed London and Confederate States Bank, it is assumed that the recognition of the southern States must ultimately, if not even very shortly, be an accomplished fact.

It is, therefore, thought desirable that preliminary measures should at once be taken to form an establishment, which will be prepared to commence operations on the resumption of trade.

It is confidently felt and openly asserted that every effort will be made by the mercantile community of the south to carry on their financial and export operations entirely independent of previously existing channels, and that New York will cease to be the medium through which shipments and financial business has hitherto been conducted.

Norfolk, from the excellence of its harbor, facility of approach, depth of water, and salubrity of its position, will afford equal, if not superior, advantages to New York, and will likely take the lead for passenger traffic and postal arrangements with mail steamers.

Wilmington, Charleston, Mobile, and Savannah offer the readier and cheaper despatch of the more bulky articles, as cotton, grain, &c., &c., whilst New Orleans will continue to forward the huge supplies floated down the Mississippi.

A further encouragement for the immediate prosecution of a scheme of this nature is to be found in the hope and expectation that any assistance and countenance given to the Confederate States before their internal troubles have terminated will, at a future time, tend to cement those good feelings which are so strongly entertained towards them, and which so many in this country earnestly desire should be mutual.

DIPLOMATIC CORRESPONDENCE, 1864

Lord Wharncliffe to Ambassador Adams:

Wortley Hall, Sheffield, November 12, 1864

Your Excellency: A bazaar has been held in St. George's Hall, Liverpool, to provide a fund for the relief of southern prisoners of war; it has produced a clear sum of about £17,000. In preference to any attempt to reach the intended object by circuitous means, a committee of English gentlemen has been formed to address you on the subject.

As chairman of this committee, I venture to ask your excellency to request the permission of your government that an accredited agent may be sent out to visit the military prisons within the northern States, and minister to the comfort of those for whom this fund is intended, under such supervision as your government may direct.

Permit me to state that no political end is aimed at by this movement. It has received support from many who were opposed to the political action of the south. Nor is it intended to impute that the confederate prisoners are denied such attentions as the ordinary rules enjoin. But these rules are narrow and stern. Winter is at hand, and the clothing which may satisfy the rules of war will not protect the natives of a warm climate from the severe cold of the north.

Sir, the issue of this great contest will not be determined by individual suffering, be it greater or less, and you, whose family name is interwoven with American history, cannot view with indifference the sufferings of American citizens, whatever their state or their opinions.

236

On more than one occasion, aid has been proffered by the people of one country to special classes under great affliction in another. May it not be permitted to us to follow these examples, especially when those we desire to solace are beyond the reach of their immediate kinsmen. I trust that these precedents and the voice of humanity may plead with your excellency, and induce you to prefer to the government of the United States the request which I have the honor to submit.

I am, sir, your obedient, humble servant,

Wharncliffe

DIPLOMATIC CORRESPONDENCE, 1865

DEATH OF GENERAL STUART

The following passages from Heros von Borcke's fascinating *Memoirs* cover the period from summer, 1863 to spring of 1864 and include a touching description of the death of Jeb Stuart on May 11, 1864.

The morning of the 19th dawned with all the bright beauty of the month of June, but the rising of the sun was also the signal for the recommencement of hostilities, and before we had had time to breakfast a rapid succession of cannon-shots summoned us to the front. The General and his Staff soon became a target for the Federal sharpshooters who, by the cheering, had become well aware that Stuart was in that small group of officers. Being dressed in the same fashion as the General—a short jacket and grey hat with waving ostrich plume, and mounted on my handsome new charger—I was mistaken for him, and my tall figure soon engaged their particular attention, for the bullets came humming around me like a swarm of bees. A ball had just stripped the gold lace from my trousers and I was saying to the General, riding a few steps before me, "General, those Yankees are giving it rather hotly to me on your account," when I suddenly felt a severe blow, as though somebody had struck me with his fist on my neck, fiery sparks glittered before my eyes and a tremendous weight seemed to be dragging me from my horse. After a few moments of insensibility, I opened my eyes again to find myself lying on the ground, my charger beside me, and a number of officers and men pressing around and endeavouring to raise me. My left arm hung stiff and lifeless, and the blood was spouting from a large wound on the side of my neck and streaming from my mouth at every breath. . . . I was conveyed to Dr. Eliason's house, where a bed was put up for me in the parlour. One after the other all my comrades dropped in during the afternoon, and seeing my face and neck swollen and disfigured by an accumulation of air, I could see by their expression that they believed me dead already and could hear the doctor answer the repeated question, "Is he alive yet?" with "Yes, but he will not live over the night." At last Stuart himself came and, bending over me, he kissed my forehead, and I felt two tears drop upon my cheek as I heard him say, "Poor fellow, your fate is a sad one, and it was for me that you received this mortal wound."

When, in later times, I stood by his own deathbed, these friendly words came vividly before my recollection. The following morning found me, to the astonishment and delight of the doctor and my comrades, not only alive, but wonderfully refreshed and strengthened by my long sleep. The battle seemed raging in the immediate vicinity and the shells bursting right over the village, when, to my great joy, my Prussian friend Captain Scheibert entered my room. At the first news of my misfortune, he had hastened from the distant headquarters of our army, bringing along General Longstreet's private ambulance, which the latter had placed at my disposal.

Spring, 1864: On the morning of the 11th May, 1864, Richmond was thrown once more into a state of excitement by the rapid advance against it of the Federal cavalry under General Sheridan who had managed to march round our lines. A road was pointed out to me with such assurance that it would take me to General Stuart without bringing me into collision with the Yankees, that I galloped along it with very little precaution. A scattered band of Federal cavalry bore down upon me, firing their revolvers and demanding my surrender. An exciting chase ensued for several miles till it was put a stop to by the fire of our pickets, whom I reached completely exhausted, and thoroughly surprised at my escape. The rapid run and the excitement of my pursuit had proved too much for my strength, and I was carried, half-fainting, to bed. After a long and refreshing sleep, I was awakened about daybreak by the voice of Dr. Brewer, Stuart's brother-in-law, who informed me that my General had been wounded severely and carried during the night to his place, where he was anxious to see me. I hastened to the bedside of my dear friend, whom I found in a small room of the Doctor's house, surrounded by most of his Staff. He received me with a smile, saying, "I'm glad you've come, my dear Von; you see they've got me at last, but don't feel uneasy. I don't think I'm so badly wounded as you were, and I hope I shall get over it as you did."

Towards noon, however, a change took place for the worse and our fears began to be greatly excited. About this time President Davis visited the prostrate hero; taking his hand, the President said, "General, how do you feel?" He replied, "Easy, but willing to die if God and my country think I have fulfilled my destiny and done my duty." As evening approached mortification set in and no hopes could any longer be entertained. He became delirious, and his mind wandered over the battle-fields where he had fought, then to his wife and children, and again to the front. Mrs. Stuart was absent with her children in the country, and several messages had been despatched informing her of her husband's state, and urging her instant return to Richmond; and in the intervals of relief from pain and delirium, the General frequently inquired if she had not yet come, beginning now to doubt the possibility of his recovery. About five o'clock the General asked Dr. Brewer how long he thought it possible he could live and whether he could survive through the night; and being told that death was rapidly approaching, he nodded, and said, "I am resigned, if it be God's will; but I should like to see my wife. But God's will be done." He then made his last dispositions and took leave of us all, I being the last.

I had been sitting on his bed, holding his hand in mine, and handing him the ice, which he ate in great abundance and which was applied to his burning hot wounds to cool them. Drawing me towards him and grasping my hand firmly, he said, "My dear Von, I am sinking fast now, but before I die I want you to know that I never loved a man as much as yourself. I pray your life may be long and happy; look after my family after I'm gone and be the same true friend to my wife and children that you have been to me." These were the last connected words he spoke. On the evening of the 13th, in the midst of the roaring of the enemy's cannon, which reached us from Drewry's Bluff, we carried Stuart's remains to the beautiful cemetery at Hollywood, near Richmond, where he lies in a simple grave by the side of his beloved little daughter Flora. Of a calm summer evening I frequently rode out to this quiet spot, sitting for hours on my leader's grave, recalling his excellent qualities and musing over the many glorious battles through which we had fought side by side.

As winter approached, a proposal already mooted several times—namely, that of sending me abroad on Government duty, but which, till then, I had always refused, hoping soon to be able to go into active campaigning—was renewed. There being very little chance of active service during the cold weather, and General Hampton, General Lee and President Davis urging me to go on a mission for the Government to England, I at last yielded to their wishes, hoping to be back for the spring campaign. My commanding

241

officer had in the meantime urgently requested that my rank should be raised to that of Colonel, and the day before my departure I had the gratification of receiving my promotion from the hands of the President. . . . I arrived in England, after a circuitous route by the West India Islands, in the month of February, 1865. There I was saved the grief of being an eyewitness of the rapid collapse of the Confederacy, and the downfall of a just and noble cause.

Lee's glorious army is no longer in existence: the brave men who formed it have, after innumerable sufferings and privations, bowed to the enemy's power and numbers, and dispersed to follow peaceful pursuits. But those who have survived the fearful struggle for independence can look back upon a series of battles and victories unequalled in history; and every one of us will for ever speak with pride of the time when he was a soldier of the army of Northern Virginia. I myself am still an invalid. The ball which I carry in my lungs gives me frequent suffering, and has broken my once so robust health; but as every renewal of my pains reminds me of the past they are alleviated and almost effaced by the pleasure with which I revert to the time when I fought side by side with those brave men; and I shall ever rejoice that I drew my sword for the gallant people of the late Confederacy.

Heros von Borcke,

MEMOIRS OF THE CONFEDERATE WAR FOR INDEPENDENCE

"CAN WE MAKE THESE MEN OUR FRIENDS"

From a speech by John Bright in
Parliament, June 30, 1863:

Every year there are one hundred and fifty thousand
children born into the world—born with the badge
and the doom of slavery—born to the liability by law,
and by custom, and by the devilish cupidity of man
—to the lash and to the chain and to the branding-
iron, and to be taken from their families and carried
they know not where.

I want to know whether you feel as I feel upon
this question. When I can get down to my home from
this House, I find half a dozen little children playing
upon my hearth. How many members are there who
cannot say with me that the most innocent, the most
pure, the most holy joy which in their past years they
have felt, or in their future years they have hoped
for, has arisen from contact and association with our
precious children? Well, then, if that be so—if, when
the hand of Death takes one of those flowers from
our dwelling, our heart is overwhelmed with sorrow
and our household is covered with gloom; what
would it be if our children were brought up to this
infernal system—one hundred and fifty thousand of

them every year brought into the world in these Slave States, amongst these *gentlemen,* amongst this *chivalry,* amongst these *men that we can make our friends?*

George Macaulay Trevelyan, LIFE OF JOHN BRIGHT

A RUSSIAN DIPLOMAT REPORTS

Baron de Stoeckl comments on the draft riots to Prince Gortchakov, Minister for Foreign Affairs at St. Petersburg:

1863

The diplomatic corps is, as last year, in an embarrassing position. I have taken all precautions to put our archives in a place of safety in case of danger and I shall take with me the most important papers of the imperial legation. . . .

New York, the metropolis of the nation, with a population of nearly 1,000,000, has been the scene of disorders more than once, but never before to such a degree as this. For the first time the people rose up against the duly constituted authorities. A mob invaded the main recruiting office, drove out the officers and set fire to the police station. Several men were killed by the troops who interceded. The government

244

is very uneasy and has ordered the suspension of recruiting at Philadelphia, where riots are also feared. . . .

The republican form of government so much talked about by the Europeans and so much praised by the Americans is breaking down. Democracy in the United States has become irresponsible, owing to the rising streams of radicalism and universal suffrage at home, to the influx of socialists and anarchists from Europe, and to the rise of such men as Garibaldi and Bakunin. What can be expected from a country where men of humble origin are elevated to the highest positions, where honest men refuse to vote and dishonest ones cast their ballots at the bidding of the shameless politicians? This is democracy in practice, the democracy that the European theorists rave about. If they could only see it at work they would cease their agitation and thank God for the government which they are enjoying.

All the adventurous spirits that there were—all the unemployed in the great cities—immigrants brought here from Europe by poverty, have been absorbed by the army. Next, conscription will draft the agricultural, industrial and commercial classes. Only force will be able to drag men of these groups away from their homes, and it is doubtful whether they will submit willingly to it. Congress has already discussed this question. Several measures have been proposed, but none has been judged practicable. In the ultimate, conscription will have to be enforced, no matter how unpopular it may be.

However, with the almost limitless powers which the federal government possesses it will manage to surmount these obstacles up to a certain point, and the war will be prolonged still further, intensifying the poverty and bloodshed which have overwhelmed this country for three years.

Albert Woldman, LINCOLN AND THE RUSSIANS

THE GAIETIES THAT WERE GOING ON

FitzGerald Ross, an Englishman, was educated at Heidelberg and Göttingen and became a professional cavalry officer in the Austrian Hussars. Like so many other well-born Europeans with military background who formed a sort of roving officer class in the armies of Europe, Ross's sympathies were inevitably drawn to the South. He spent one year with the Confederate Army, and in his diary he reveals an ardent, pro-South, pro-slavery attitude.

Charleston, S.C., September, 1863

We made several more excursions into the country during our stay at Charleston, and as the planters take great pleasure in showing and telling us all about their plantations, I had a pretty good opportunity of seeing the working of their system. The "hands," who have each and all a cottage allotted to them, with a "patch" to raise corn and vegetables and poultry, show every external sign of material happiness. They are well fed and well clothed, and sport as much finery on Sundays, and are as fond of doing so, as a millowner's "hands" in England.

They are singularly attached to their masters, who invariably treat them with the greatest kindness. No clergyman's wife in England can be more conscientious in visiting the sick and aged amongst her husband's parishioners, reading the Bible to them, and furnishing them with medicine and little comforts, than are the ladies in the South in administering to the wants of the helpless amongst their own people. To exercise charity in this way is taught them as one of their first duties. That there is no disposition on the part of the Negroes to rebel against the present system, has been clearly shown in the course of this war. At the commencement, many—wiled away by false representations, and foolishly thinking that the freedom promised them by the Yankees meant a total exemption from labour for all future time—did certainly run away and take refuge with the Yankees; but they have, most of them, bitterly repented of their mistake, and many have returned whenever they could find an opportunity. The Yankees "liberate" a great many, sorely against their will, wherever they penetrate, but that is to make soldiers of them. . . . To emancipate the Negroes now, as the Abolitionists propose, would be an act of the greatest cruelty towards them, and would certainly in the end result in their extermination, just as the Red Indians, a far nobler race, have perished before them.

Richmond now presented a very different aspect
from what it had done in summer. Congress, as well
as the State Legislature of Virginia, was in session; the
shops were full of stores, and crowded with pur-
chasers; hosts of furloughed officers and soldiers per-
ambulated the streets; hotels, restaurants, and bar-
rooms were crowded with guests, and the whole city
presented a lively appearance.

There was some outcry, even from the pulpits,
against the gaieties that were going on, but General
Lee was reported to have said that the young ladies
were quite right to afford the officers and soldiers
on furlough as much amusement as possible; and
balls, *tableaux vivants,* and all kinds of social gatherings, were the order of the day.

Gambling, however, as an unmitigated vice, has
lately been checked by the Virginia Legislature. They
debated a little whether to legalise gambling, and by
making it a public amusement to check gamblers by
public opinion, or whether to put it down by severe
measures, and decided for the latter. All gamblers
caught in the fact were to be heavily fined, and the
banker to be flogged. Corporal punishment is not
otherwise generally popular in this country. . . .

Richmond, January, 1864

Congress, in both houses, has been voting thanks
to the generals and armies, and, what we all thought
an especially graceful act, both houses gave a particular vote of thanks to Major von Borcke, a Prussian
officer who has done gallant service under General

Stuart, and was very severely wounded during the Pennsylvania campaign.

There are very few foreigners in the Confederate service. . . . The Yankee service, on the other hand, is crowded with adventurers. Not only was the North easy of access, but, from having been for a long time the receptacle of the "scum and refuse of Europe," most of the revolutionary heroes of 1848 and later, such as Blenker, were there already.

In European armies numberless officers are obliged to quit their profession, mostly from having been extravagant; and to these "soldiers of fortune" the American war has been a perfect godsend. They have all espoused the Northern cause, not because it was dearest, but because it was nearest to them. Many of them are excellent officers. The Southern Confederacy being very difficult of access, the foreigners who have taken service here have all been impelled to do so by their sympathy with the cause, which is in truth a noble one. Very few foreign officers even visit the Southern States now, which surprises me, for nothing could exceed the courtesy and kindness with which strangers are received; and so interesting a period of seeing the country can hardly be expected to occur again.

Fredericksburg, January, 1864

On the 9th of January I accompanied General Stuart on a tour of inspection to see some of his brigades near Fredericksburg. . . . The Mayor of Fredericksburg—who possesses, what is remarkable since the battles last year, an entire house, with furniture in it—entertained us hospitably, and in the evening we went to a ball.

Fredericksburg, which, before the war, is said to have been a delightful residence, has undergone manifold misfortunes in the last two years. After having been in Yankee hands in the summer of 1862, it suffered a terrible ordeal in December of that year, when the battle took place to which it gives its name. It was bombarded for hours together, after which the Yankees took possession; and finally, before leaving, they totally pillaged it. Again, during the battle of Chancellorsville, the enemy got possession, and again they pillaged it. It is still so near the Yankee lines that, although safe at present, it may at any moment be subjected to the tender mercies of their armies. Consequently, although the inhabitants have returned to their homes, they are by no means as particular as they used to be about having good furniture, and everything nice and stylish about them. In the ball-room, at the private houses where we danced, there was very little furniture besides the piano, and it was illuminated by tallow-candles stuck into empty black bottles. Perhaps some of the ladies may have been dressed in homespun instead of silks and satins —but it was too dark to see. For all that, we had as pleasant a party as could possibly be; and were very sorry when twelve o'clock came and put an end to the ball, as the next day was Sunday.

On leaving—there had been none but young ladies there, no chaperones—every young lady paired off with a gentleman who accompanied her to her home. Unacquainted with the customs of the country, I was left out in the cold without a partner, much to Stuart's amusement. This was a new experience, although I had seen and admired before the independence which young ladies are allowed in America.

Mobile had suffered very little from the war, and still carried on a brisk commerce with the outer world in spite of the blockade.

We took up our quarters at the Battle House, an enormous caravanserai; and after a refreshing bath, and a capital breakfast at a French restaurant, we sallied forth for a walk in the city.

In the evening we went to a grand wedding-party and ball, where all the beauty of Mobile was assembled; and the reports I had heard of the charms of the fair sex at Mobile I found to be not at all exaggerated. This was the last ball of the season, as Lent was about to commence, but they had been very gay here during the carnival. There is always a great deal of social intercourse at Mobile, and I shall ever cherish amongst my most agreeable recollections of the South the pleasant hours spent with the genial inhabitants of that city.

One day we went down the bay to visit the outer defences in a magnificent river-steamer. The Governor of Alabama, Admiral Buchanan, General Maury, and other gentlemen and ladies, were of the party. A very good band of music from one of the regiments of the garrison played, and dancing was soon got up in the splendid saloon. They dance the "finale" of the quadrille here with all sorts of figures—one of them like the last figure in the Lancers, walking round and giving the right and left hand alternately. Admiral Buchanan, who was looking on, joined in this, and naturally by doing so created a great deal of confusion and merriment, at which he was in high glee. He is immensely popular, and the young ladies all call him a charming old gentleman, although he is at least ten years too young to be an admiral in England.

I was present at Mobile at two weddings; one was that of General Tom Taylor, and the other of my friend Colonel von Scheliha with Miss Williams, upon which occasion I officiated as groomsman. On the day this ceremony took place, we heard that nine other couples had been wedded. The happy men were all officers in the army. They say that marriages were never more frequent in the South than now. General Stuart was a great promoter of matches. He used to tell his officers that now was their time; they could marry without any questions being asked as to how they could support their wives, who would naturally remain at their homes and be taken care of by their parents. If they waited till the war was over it would be different. It was, to be sure, shockingly improvident, but seeing difficulties far ahead was not a foible of Stuart's.

FitzGerald Ross, CITIES AND CAMPS OF THE CONFEDERATE STATES

"I HAVE NO DISLIKE OF THE NEGROES"

Thomas Carlyle was educated for the ministry but ultimately abandoned it to become one of England's greatest historians and the author of the classic, *The French Revolution*. As the leading social critic of his time his influence was felt by such contemporaries as John Ruskin and Matthew Arnold. Among his many American friends and correspondents was Moncure David Conway, a clergyman who was also the editor of the works of Tom Paine and the author of biographies of Carlyle, Emerson and Hawthorne. Born the son of a Virginia slave-owner, his early views on slavery were those of his class, but by the time he attained his first pulpit his sermons carried such a strong anti-slavery message that President Lincoln sent him to Europe to preach in behalf of the Northern cause. The following excerpts are from letters written by Carlyle to Conway in the period 1863–1864.

Nothing I ever witnessed so fills me with astonishment and sorrow as the present condition of things in America. . . . I see it all as fire rained out of the heavens.

I have no dislike of the Negroes. By wise and kindly treatment they might have been made into a happy and contented labouring population. I do not wish for them any condition which I would not, under like circumstances, wish for myself.

253

The America for which you are hoping, you will never see, and you will never see the whites and blacks in the South dwelling together as equals in peace.

Moncure D. Conway, AUTOBIOGRAPHY

FOR PEACE IN AMERICA

Under the heading, "The People of the United Kingdom of Great Britain and Ireland to the People of the United States of America," the following petition calling for a cessation of hostilities was circulated in England and Ireland. "When this unfortunate war began, our hearts were more inclined towards you than towards your sister States, because we believed with you that the action of the South was but the work of a fraction," it says in part and then continues with expressions of disappointment in the North and support of the South.

We are of the same race, and many of you are our brothers. We, therefore, come to you as peace-makers, and address you in plain language as friends and as fellow-men. We ask you, has there not been enough of strife and bloodshed, of misery and suffering; and is it not time to cease the cruel war in which you are engaged?

When you asserted that secession was the work of disappointed ambition, and promised to quell it within sixty days, we accepted your assurances in good faith, looking for the speedy restoration of peace, for we did not wish to see the American Union broken up.

But so far from this promise being fulfilled . . . peace and the restoration of the Union are apparently as distant as ever.

The events of the struggle have convinced us that a more united people never rose up in defence of their rights than those of the southern States. Surely there must be many now among you who share with us the conviction that it has become utterly impossible to subdue the south, or to restore the American Union as it existed in the past days of the republic. . . .

We believe that the war has changed (for the present at least) the character of your government. It has swept away your freedom of speech, your free press, and the inestimable right of habeas corpus.

We believe that the southern people are only following the precepts and example taught and practiced by your fathers and theirs, when they withdrew their allegiance from the mother country, and that the Declaration of Independence, which you hallow and celebrate every fourth day of July, asserts, as self-evident, the right of the southern people to set up a government of their own.

We believe that *should you, at the end of another three and a half years' war, succeed in subduing the south and restoring the union by force of arms, you* will find out, when it is too late, that those pillars upon which rests your republican form of government have been violently torn down, and that your own liberties have been buried in the ruins. We ask you to compare the course pursued by the south now and the colonies in 1776, with that adopted by the north now and the mother country then, and we think you will discover many striking resemblances.

It is in your hands to give peace to the American continent. The southern States have appealed to you for peace, and to be let alone.

We appeal to you to . . . make peace with the southern States; and we make this appeal in the name of religion, humanity, civilization, and common justice.

DIPLOMATIC CORRESPONDENCE, 1864

A RUSSIAN DIPLOMAT REPORTS

Baron de Stoeckl, Russian Ambassador at Washington, to Prince Gortchakov, Minister for Foreign Affairs at St. Petersburg:

1864

We find ourselves again in the same danger which we ran into two years ago. The city is in a state of consternation. The President and the members of the Cabinet have a gunboat ready to take them away if the Confederates should succeed in entering the city. We cannot hope that the government, in case of danger, will assume responsibility for the diplomatic corps, and we shall have to provide our own means of reaching safety.

Albert Woldman, LINCOLN AND THE RUSSIANS

LETTER FROM PROSPER MÉRIMÉE
TO EDWARD LEE CHILDE

February 13, 1864

I was hoping you would give me some news of the Charlestown siege. It seems that the South is very weak and the North gaining a lot of ground, which doesn't imply in the least that they shine because of their common sense, their magnanimity or for any other virtue except, perhaps, tenacity. The people of Aragon were said to drive nails with their heads; this same delightful exertion could be applied to the Yankees.

Maurice Parturier, ed., COLLECTED LETTERS OF PROSPER MÉRIMÉE

London, May 3, 1864—The present prospects of the Confederates in this fourth year of the war are brighter than ever.

THE TIMES

"MY HEART GOES WITH THE SOUTH, AND MY HEAD WITH THE NORTH"

Scientist and philosopher, Thomas Henry Huxley influenced English thought by his many speeches and writings on philosophical and religious matters. The following letter was written to his sister, a Mrs. Scott, who had lived in America for years and whose fifteen-year-old son was fighting with the Confederates.

May 5, 1864

I have read all you tell me about the south with much interest and with the warmest sympathy, so far as the fate of the south affects you. But I am in the condition of most thoughtful Englishmen. My heart goes with the south, and my head with the north.

I have no love for the Yankees, and I delight in the energy and self-sacrifice of your people; but for all that, I cannot doubt that whether you beat the Yankees or not, you are struggling to uphold a system which must, sooner or later, break down.

I have not the smallest sentimental sympathy with the Negro; don't believe in him at all, in short. But it is clear to me that slavery means, for the white man, bad political economy; bad social morality; bad internal political organization, and a bad influence upon free labor and freedom all over the world. For the sake of the white man, therefore, for your children and grandchildren, directly, and for mine, indirectly, I wish to see this system ended. Would that the south had had the wisdom to initiate that end without this miserable war!

All this must jar upon you sadly, and I grieve that it does so; but I could not pretend to be other than I am, even to please you. Let us agree to differ upon this point. If I were in your place I doubt not I should feel as you do; and, when I think of you, I put myself in your place and feel with you as your brother Tom. The learned gentleman who has public opinions for which he is responsible to another "party" who walks about in T's clothes when he is not thinking of his sister.

If this were not my birthday I should not feel justified in taking a morning's holiday to write this long letter to you. The ghosts of undone pieces of work are dancing about me, and I must come to an end.

Give my love to your husband. I am glad to hear he wears so well. And don't forget to give your children kindly thought of their uncle. Dr. Wright gives a great account of my namesake, and says he is the handsomest youngster in the Southern States. . . .

Leonard Huxley, LIFE AND LETTERS OF THOMAS HENRY HUXLEY

NOTES FROM THE BELGIAN PRESS

May 27, 1864—At no time have we seen combats more bloody and more sterile! We have always thought that the flow of blood calms little by little the wrath of men. Here, on the contrary, the more blood flows, the more seems to mount the fury of the combattants. All can be explained. An enormous outrage was committed before God by the Americans —those who tolerated and those who practiced slavery. This is a great expiation that we are watching.

COURRIER DE L'ESCAUT

TWELVE FRENCH PATRIOTS OF TOURS

John Slidell figured prominently in the Trent Affair when Jefferson Davis appointed him Confederate Commissioner to France in 1861. When the excitement of the Affair died down Slidell proceeded to Paris early in

1862. He was hospitably received there but was never able to win official recognition or get any material help from France. The following letter was sent to him in 1864 by twelve French citizens.

To M. Slidell
Commissioner of the Confederate States of America

Sir:

We admit your countrymen are brave; that they are chivalrous to one another, loyal to their chiefs, capable of patriotic enthusiasm, of undergoing hardships, *But—do they support slavery?*

We do not deny to the Southern people personal honor, magnanimity, self-respect and intelligence, *But—do they keep their fellow men in a degrading servitude because of their color?*

We, Frenchmen, grant beauty, grace and chastity to your women, *But—before we render them our homage, we ask, do they own slaves?*

So far from denying your right to political freedom, to choose your own government, to resist oppression, we approve and would aid you with all our power, *But—before we move one single inch, we must insist on your reply to this question: Do you mean to uphold slavery? Do you still refuse freedom to the slaves?*

Until you can answer this question, dear Mr. Slidell, and answer it in one way, it is useless to make any appeal to the people of France. It may be to our interest to support you. There may be strong mate-

rial and political reasons for a close alliance between
us, but as long as you maintain and are maintained
by slavery, we cannot offer you our alliance. On the
contrary, we believe and expect you will fail!

Twelve French Patriots of Tours

Beckles Willson, JOHN SLIDELL AND THE CONFEDERATES IN PARIS

HYPOCRISY IN THE NORTH

Duvergier de Hauranne was a well-
known French political figure and a
frequent contributor to the *Revue des
Deux Mondes.* Between 1864–1865 he
spent eight months traveling in America and the result was a volume called
*Eight Months in America: Letters and
Travel Notes,* from which this is an
excerpt.

New York, June 20, 1864

Between Broadway and the Hudson River there
exists a filthy, rundown neighborhood inhabited by
Irish immigrants and colored people exclusively. It
is impossible to imagine anything more depressingly
poor than these wooden shacks and long muddy
avenues. From time to time one sees with amazement

a trolley car ride by which carries a sign: "Colored People Admitted." What in the world can be the meaning of this? Are we in Illinois? Are there separate laws here for Negroes? No, but public prejudice persecutes them more powerfully, more tyrannically even than law. Colored people are thrown off buses and driven out of churches. That is how these democrats conceive equality, these Puritans, Christian charity. Southern Catholics at least admit Negroes to their churches; but the Northerners who are supposed to be liberating them do not even consider them their equals in the eye of God. Is it true then that slavery constitutes for the North nothing but a pretext and that its abolition is in reality a war machine? This would still not be enough to justify the decision of the people in the South to take up arms in defense of an odious prejudice; but if principles are being used by the people of the North merely as an ingenious mask to conceal their true ambitions, it is hard not to show mistrust of something which so closely resembles hypocrisy. . . .

It is not possible to continue treating like dogs those whom we call our brothers or to forbid those whom we consider worthy to serve their country to worship God in the same churches as we do.

Duvergier de Hauranne, LETTERS AND TRAVEL NOTES

MARX-ENGELS

CORRESPONDENCE CONTINUED

Marx to Engels:

September 7, 1864

Lincoln has in his hands great resources with which to carry this election. (Peace proposals on his part are naturally mere humbug!) The election of an opposition candidate would probably lead to a real *revolution*. But all the same one cannot fail to recognize that for the coming eight weeks, in which the issue will in the first instance be decided, much depends on military accident. This is absolutely the most critical point since the beginning of the war. If this is shifted, old Lincoln can then blunder on to his heart's content. For the rest, the old man cannot possibly "make" generals. He could already choose his ministers better. . . . If Lincoln gets through this time—as is very probable—it will be on a much more radical platform and under wholly changed circumstances. In conformity with his legal manner, the old man will then find more radical methods compatible with his conscience.

Marx and Engels, THE CIVIL WAR IN THE UNITED STATES

NOTES FROM THE BELGIAN PRESS

November 25, 1864—The London *Times* has received news from the United States dated the 9th and 10th of November which smacks as usual of the Southern sources from which it is drawn and consequently crawls with contradictions. . . .

The re-election of Mr. Lincoln to the presidency of the United States arouses strange rage within the camp of the Southern parties in England. The *Times* . . . carried away by the ardor of its Southern sympathies, sees nothing less in the results of the presidential election than "the first episode of the foundation of a tyranny upon the ruins of the free government of the United States." These exaggerations are just ridiculous and it suffices simply to point them out; the good sense of the public will quickly dispose of them. . . .

The military situation has never been so good for the Federal army as it is at this time and if ever it has been permitted to hope for the quick and complete defeat of the secession, it is surely in the present circumstances, when the Northern government, strengthened by the new elections, reaffirmed in its authority, fortified in its action, will be able to give to its operations an impulse even more energetic than in the past.

INDEPENDENCE BELGE

PERSEVERE, ILLUSTRIOUS

PRESIDENT!

> The democratic party of Barcelona
> sends a congratulatory message to
> President Lincoln upon his re-elec-
> tion, December 6, 1864:

*To the citizen Abraham Lincoln, President of
the republic of the United States:*

> This event proves that the grand idea—cause of the
> grandest war which the annals of the world record—
> existed not alone in the mind of one man, but in the
> consciences of a whole people, proves that the Presi-
> dent's proclamation for the abolition of slavery well
> expressed the noble aspiration of the people of the
> United States, who could no longer sustain so un-
> worthy an inheritance under a flag in whose shadow
> do battle justice against iniquity, liberty against
> servitude, morality against the most horrible crime.
>
> Youthful America regards with consternation your
> fields soaked with blood and old Europe shudders
> with anguish. What matter? Your idea is superior to
> all. . . . The good, the honorable of all countries are
> with you and with the people you lead victorious in
> the noble strife.

Persevere, illustrious President, in your work: and when the solemn hour of your complete triumph shall sound, let the abolition of slavery in the United States be the signal for the abolition of all slavery among mankind.

DIPLOMATIC CORRESPONDENCE, 1865

A RUSSIAN DIPLOMAT REPORTS

Baron de Stoeckl, Russian Ambassador in Washington, to Prince Gortchakov, Minister for Foreign Affairs at St. Petersburg:

1865:

One of the characteristics of this nation is its confidence in itself, in its destiny, and in its belief that "the best government that God ever saw will last forever."

Albert Woldman, LINCOLN AND THE RUSSIANS

PROSPER MÉRIMÉE

CORRESPONDENCE CONTINUED

February 1, 1865

To Edward Lee Childe:

Your friend Abraham seems to me to be winning all along the line. I believe that your uncle will be defeated this year and that the English and ourselves will look on without lifting a finger, only to deplore later not having joined in when it was still time. The conquest of the South may make a lot of trouble for the North. It's all very well to cut your cloth, but you must afterward sew the pieces together again, as Catherine de Médici used to say. It's more than likely that your abominable fellow citizens, having acquired both the taste and the experience of war will indulge in this new pastime by hurling themselves on Canada and Mexico, grabbing Cuba and getting us generally into all sorts of difficulties. Your Yankees have something of the stupidity and singleness of purpose of the Romans. . . .

To Sir Anthony Panizzi, an Italian patriot who had escaped arrest in his country by taking refuge in England where he eventually became chief librarian of the British Museum:

April 22, 1865

Now that the Confederates have been driven to the wall, what remains to be done is to pacify the country, and how Mr. Lincoln is going to set about such a task is what I would like to see. What with a House of Representatives made up of scoundrels and a Senate presided over by a tailor who is also a complete drunkard, who can tell what mad things we'll witness? The worst part of the business is that these rascals are in reality very powerful and they show themselves on every occasion as obstinate as mules and as totally devoid of any scruples of conscience as your little sixteenth-century Italian tyrants were. . . .

Maurice Parturier, ed., COLLECTED LETTERS OF PROSPER MÉRIMÉE

A REMINDER FROM
THE BRITISH FOREIGN OFFICE

Lord Russell notifies Messers Mason, Slidell and Mann, the Confederate agents in Europe, that Her Majesty's government will put up with no further nonsense from these gentlemen or the "so-called confederate government" they represent.

Foreign Office, February 13, 1865

Gentlemen: Some time ago I had the honor to inform you, in answer to a statement which you sent me, that her Majesty remained neutral in the deplorable contest now carried on in North America, and that her Majesty intended to persist in that course.

It is now my duty to request you to bring to the notice of the authorities under whom you act, the just complaints which her Majesty's government have to make of the conduct of the so-called confederate government. The facts upon which these complaints are founded tend to show that her Majesty's neutrality is not respected by the agents of that government, and that undue and reprehensible attempts have been made by them to involve her Majesty in a war in which her Majesty had declared her intention not to take part.

In the first place, I am sorry to observe that the unwarrantable practice of building ships in this country to be used as vessels of war against a state with whom her Majesty is at peace still continues. Her Majesty's government had hoped that this attempt to make the territorial waters of Great Britain the place of preparation for warlike armaments against the United States might be put an end to by prosecutions and by seizure of the vessels built in pursuance of contracts made with the confederate agents. But facts which are, unhappily, too notorious, and correspondence which has been put into the hands of her Majesty's government by the minister of the government of the United States, show that resort is had to evasion and subtlety, in order to escape the penalties of the law; that a vessel is bought in one place, that her armament is prepared in another, and that both are sent to some distant port beyond her Majesty's jurisdiction, and that thus an armed steamship is fitted out to cruise against the commerce of a power in amity with her Majesty. A crew composed partly of British subjects is procured separately; wages are paid to them for an unknown service. They are despatched, perhaps, to the coast of France, and there or elsewhere are engaged to serve in a confederate man-of-war.

Now, it is very possible that by such shifts and stratagems the penalties of the existing law of this country, nay, of any law that could be enacted, may be evaded; but the offence thus offered to her Majesty's authority and dignity by the de facto rulers of the Confederate States, whom her Majesty acknowledges as belligerents, and whose agents in the United Kingdom enjoy the benefit of our hospitality in quiet security, remains the same. It is a proceeding totally unjustifiable and manifestly offensive to the British crown. . . .

I trust that you will feel yourselves authorized to promise, on behalf of the confederate government, that practices so offensive and unwarrantable shall cease, and shall be entirely abandoned for the future.

Russell

DIPLOMATIC CORRESPONDENCE, 1866

A NOBLE PAGE

IN THE HISTORY OF GREAT MEN

Letter from the Bishop of Orléans, Monsignor Dupanloup, to his friend Augustin Cochin. As early as 1861 Cochin had published a book, *The Abolition of Slavery,* which was considered the most important work on the subject at that time. Cochin was also a well-known pamphleteer and the author of many articles on the political and social problems of the day. In the letter which follows the Bishop tells Cochin how deeply moved he was after reading Lincoln's Second Inaugural Address.

March 4, 1865

. . . I have read this document with deep religious emotion and with profoundly sympathetic admiration. Whatever the fluctuations and the political involvements of this grave American question may be, I, as Catholic Bishop, must hope, and do desire with all my heart to see this lamentable civil war ended, and peace, a peace acceptable to all, restored. But this conflict will also have had its greatness. It will have demonstrated the amazing energy of a great people; it will have given the death blow to the odious institutions of slavery; it will have caused the grandiose idea of expiation to prevail over the spirit of profit. How momentous to hear the leader of a powerful nation speaking the words of a Christian, so rarely heard here in Europe, announcing the end of slavery and showing the way to this fusion of Justice and of Mercy which is mentioned in the Holy Scriptures.

I am grateful to you for giving me the opportunity to read this noble page in the history of great men, and I beg you to kindly convey my friendliest sentiments to Mr. Bigelow. If he were to transmit them to Mr. Lincoln I should indeed feel honored.

Comte de Montalembert, LA VICTOIRE DU NORD AUX ETATS-UNIS

LETTER FROM WILLIAM HOWARD RUSSELL TO JOHN BIGELOW

March 8, 1865

I do not know what grounds Delane has for it, but he is quite sure Uncle Samuel is about to finish off the dreadful civil war by another war with us scarcely less horrible. You know perhaps that, as I from the first maintained the North must win, I was tabooed from dealing with American questions in the *Times* even after my return to England, but *en revanche* I have had my say in the *Army and Navy Gazette,* which I have bought, every week, and if one could be weak and wicked enough to seek for a morbid gratification amid such ruins and blood, I might be proud of the persistence with which I maintained my opinions against adverse and unanimous sentiment. . . .

John Bigelow, RETROSPECTIONS OF AN ACTIVE LIFE

SPANIARDS TAKE HOPE

Spain was undergoing a series of violent uprisings, military coups d'état and dictatorships during the American Civil War. The following is part of an address from the citizens of Eclhe, Spain, to President Lincoln, hailing the victories of a democratically governed nation.

Now, when unfortunate Spain is plunged in a frightful reaction; now when the enemies of liberty among ourselves occupy the places of power and regain one by one those difficult conquests which were made in the turmoil of a devastating civil war which has thus become unproductive for the cause of the people; now, when the great orators of liberty find the path

to the rostrum blocked; now, that science groans
under blows dealt in the face of most worthy men;
now, that the press is muzzled violently; now, that
again are repeated among us scenes only witnessed
when a foreign soldiery dishonored our soil and spat
in the face of the honest and brave Spanish people:
now, it is highly consolatory for us who have faith
and hope in the future and who do not doubt the
justice of God, to see that liberty does not succumb,
that progress goes on and makes its daily journey,
and that to our lot it has fallen to see the destruction
of barbarian slavery, and that it is a people democratically governed which has carried to its close the
greatest enterprise in history. The people and the
army which have made such sacrifices in so just a
cause have merited well of humanity. And the President of the republic, called by Providence to guide
so great a people in moments decisive and supreme,
will live always in the memory of coming generations,
who shall bless his name so long as justice lives upon
the earth.

DIPLOMATIC CORRESPONDENCE, 1865

WHEN DARKNESS FELL

Marquis Adolphe de Chambrun was
a trained lawyer and journalist who
departed for the United States in December of 1864 with a view to settling

in this country. With the approval of the French Foreign Ministry, he acted as unofficial observer of the war that was rapidly approaching its climax by the time he arrived. Unlike most foreign military and diplomatic envoys, Marquis de Chambrun was a staunch supporter of the Federal government. The following excepts are from letters to his wife, dated from February 27 to April 10, 1865.

When I think that they are still discussing in Europe whether or not the North will subjugate the South, I cannot really believe such folly exists and think I must be dreaming. . . . I am now acquainted with nearly all the important persons in Washington. I am everywhere treated as a warm friend who thinks as they do and with whom explanations are unnecessary. This is not at all the case with our Legation. Impossible to dream of a situation more foolish than theirs or one more impolitic. These gentlemen live among themselves, see nobody, and never speak to any native. They loudly proclaim that France made only one mistake, which is not to have immediately recognized the South and, if necessary, declared war on North America. As a commentary they add that Americans are ill-bred, the women badly dressed and what not. All this is said so publicly that it comes back to me from all sides at once. . . .

The hour of decision has struck. Two days more and the evacuation of Richmond will be an accomplished fact. President Lincoln himself has just gone to the front. . . . To my astonishment, Mrs. Lincoln, who is returning to the Army of the Potomac in company with Mr. Sumner, invited me this evening to go with them. . . . We went down the Potomac as far as the sea, then turned into Chesapeake Bay and ascended the James River up to City Point, a distance of about 450 kilometers made in twenty-four hours. President Lincoln was on his own steamer, the *River Queen,* a charming and comfortable yacht on which I passed four days. It was decided to proceed immediately to Richmond. . . .

We proceeded through the streets; on either side all the stores had been pillaged. Blinds were drawn down, shutters tightly closed. Before retreating, the Confederates had released all the convicts in order to set fire to the town. From the doorways, terrified white people peeped out; they darted angry glances toward us, but showed no other sign of hostility. The aristocracy of the place, when they had not already taken flight, remained close within doors. On all the windows the green Venetian blinds were hermetically shut.

We arrived at Jefferson Davis' mansion, now Federal Headquarters. General Weitzel, who is in command, showed us through the residence of the ex-President of the Confederacy, who had carried away everything movable in his hasty flight. But, foreseeing that his house would be used for this purpose, he had instructed the few domestics left on the spot to this effect: "Take good care of the General who will occupy my old home." . . . Words cannot describe the condition of the rooms occupied by the Confederate legislature. What dirt and confusion these last days have accumulated there! It recalls nothing human.

When darkness fell the spectacle was fearful indeed. The rebels had destroyed the gas tanks and water pipes. It was impossible to find candles in the ravaged shops. The houses were buried in obscurity. No sound of hoofs in the abandoned streets, not a single voice raised in this city of thirty thousand souls. But on the other side of the town, before us, an immense wall of fire rose into the air. . . . To sum up the situation: enthusiasm among nearly all the Negro population, satisfaction among the poor whites, and total eclipse of the landowning aristocracy. . . .

On Sunday, April 9th, we were proceeding up the Potomac. That whole day the conversation turned on literary subjects. Mr. Lincoln read aloud to us for several hours. Most of the passages he selected were from Shakespeare, especially *Macbeth*. The lines after the murder of Duncan, when the new king falls a prey to moral torment, were dramatically dwelt on. Now and then he paused to expatiate on how exact a picture Shakespeare here gives of a murderer's mind when, the dark deed achieved, its perpetrator already envies his victim's calm sleep. He read the scene over twice.

Marquis Adolphe de Chambrun,
IMPRESSIONS OF LINCOLN AND THE CIVIL WAR

MEMO TO THE QUEEN

Prince Chlodwig von Hohenlohe-Schillingsfurst, a premier of Bavaria and later ambassador to Paris, was asked by his great-aunt, Queen Victoria, for a memorandum on the political problems that were agitating the German people at the moment. Point four in his response, which was dated April 15, 1865, was the following:

The American Civil War profoundly affects the material interest of the land. It is not only our cotton-spinners who are suffering; it is a question of life and death with them. The capitalists who have put their money into American stock also are anxiously watching the progress of the War and long for the conclusion of peace and the triumph of the Northern States. Besides, the sympathies of the democratic population of South Germany are naturally with the North American States.

MEMOIRS OF PRINCE CHLODWIG VON HOHENLOHE-SCHILLINGSFURST

A BLANK PAGE FOR
WHAT CONCERNS AMERICA

At a meeting of the Corps Législatif on April 15, 1865, an amendment to an address from the crown was proposed suggesting that a message of sympathy and thanks be sent to the United States for its efforts in behalf of civil liberty. While the amendment was under discussion, the news of Lee's flight and the evacuation of Richmond reached the Chamber. Eugène Pelletan had the floor briefly but the members were in no mood to discuss Franco-American relations at such a crucial moment in American affairs and the majority preferred to take counsel before defining their position. Pelletan had intended to talk at considerable length but the news brought by the telegraph was more dramatic than anything he could say and so he contented himself with a brief amplification of the amendment which follows here. The amendment was rejected by 195–24.

I do not desire either for the Chamber or for myself to prolong the debate. I have but a word to say upon this emendation, the object of which is to make reparation for an omission. In fact, no allusion to North America is made in the address from the crown, nor in the draft of our address, nor even in the *Livre Jaune,* which contains but a blank page for what concerns America.

Now, the American question is sufficiently important to be treated with less reserve; besides, at the present time, all discussion is useless, for at this very moment while I am speaking, the victorious sound of Grant and of Sherman has decided the question.

Richmond is taken. The slaveholding rebellion is stricken to the earth, and the American republic is reinstated in its majestic unity. [Noise.] Do not laugh, gentlemen; you may be heard on the other side of the Atlantic. [Renewed noise.] For four years the United States of America have borne the weight of civil war, and never for an instant during the whole of this grievous ordeal have they entertained an idea of suspending the liberties of the people; never have they opened the door of arbitrary power through which crime so often finds a passage. [Votes! votes!] The executive authority has been allowed to protect itself by legality under the fire of the enemy. This page of American history is the most illustrious page of the nineteenth century. President Lincoln has been fully aware that he held the destinies of the New World in his hands, and he has shown himself equal to the emergency; he has abolished slavery, and he has founded a second time the glorious American republic. [The votes! The votes!]

It seems to me that wherever anything great and admirable is done, there ought France to be present. For this reason I desire to send our heartfelt felicitations to the other side of the ocean.

John Bigelow, RETROSPECTIONS OF AN ACTIVE LIFE

SIR EDWARD BULWER-LYTTON

ON LEE'S SURRENDER

April, 1865

Well, I must tell you frankly, Mr. Bigelow, I am
sorry for it. I had indulged the hope that your country might break up into two or perhaps more fragments. I regard the United States as a menace to the
whole civilized world, if you are allowed to go on
developing as you have been, undisturbed.

John Bigelow, RETROSPECTIONS OF AN ACTIVE LIFE

MAZZINI ON THE NORTHERN

VICTORY

Giuseppe Mazzini, the Italian revolutionary and patriot, sometimes called
"the prophet of modern Europe,"
made the following statement early in
1865, shortly after Lee's surrender:

You have done more for us in four years than fifty
years of teaching, preaching and writing from all
your European brothers have been able to do. . . .

Jordan and Pratt, EUROPE AND THE AMERICAN CIVIL WAR

YOUNG AMERICA'S TEACHINGS
WILL NOT BE LOST ON OLD EUROPE

Throughout Europe the news of the
fall of Richmond and the rout of General Lee was considered certain evidence of the end of the war. There was
great rejoicing in all the European
capitals, marked by immense public
gatherings and torchlight processions.
In Brussels, after a parade through
the streets preceded by music and
flags of the United States and Belgium,
a cheering crowd assembled at the
American legation on the evening of
April 22nd and presented an address
of congratulation to Ambassador Sanford. Excerpts from the address follow:

The capital of the rebels is taken; the star-spangled
banner floats over the walls of Richmond. It may be
asserted henceforth that the revolt is conquered and

that the Union will subsist in its integrity. These facts represent more than material victories, and therefore we could not remain indifferent to them.

When a country enjoys, as yours does, every liberty; when every part of its territory, when every individual, has its share in the national sovereignty, resistance to the laws of the majority is an attack upon right; armed rebellion becomes a crime. The revolt of the south against the north was unjustifiable. . . .

The blood which has been shed will not flow in vain. The dead have freed the living. Two hundred and fifty thousand men of the north have perished, but, in falling, they have given liberty, and admitted to the common law four millions of slaves, and with them a whole race up to this day oppressed and despised.

The whole world has been deeply moved by your successes, for it feels that beyond the seas you are a harbor to it. . . . It knows that with you every man is really a citizen in the true acceptation and grandeur of that word, and in the whole reality also it knows that with you all the powers emanate from the nation. These principles are not only inscribed in your Constitution—the practice of each day reaffirms them.

What marvelous results have everywhere been obtained by you! Human invention, extending each day its limits; your system of railroads and telegraphs, vaster than that of all Europe . . . popular instruction, that vivifying well-spring, penetrating from strata to strata, till it reaches the home of the poorest citizen . . . the participation in public affairs of all the citizens formed in the double school of a vigilant press, which spreads abroad everywhere the opening idea, and of immense popular assemblies, where come, and whence issue in every direction, the great currents of opinion . . . finally, even in the midst of the severest trials, this admirable spectacle of order always maintained in the midst of agitation, and of liberty ever respected.

These teachings which Young America gives us will not be lost on Old Europe. You have thus paved the way for universal brotherhood. You have strengthened the Union at home; we count upon you to cement the union of peoples.

DIPLOMATIC CORRESPONDENCE, 1866

"LOOK AND LEARN,
O YOU PEOPLE OF EUROPE"

Comte Charles de Montalembert, publicist, historian and leader of the liberal Catholic party, was a steadfast and eloquent friend of the Union. He was an advocate of the doctrine of separation of Church and State and he labored tirelessly to effect a reconciliation between the Church and modern democracy. His *La Victoire du Nord aux Etats-Unis* was a tribute to American democracy.

We were told the American people were not capable of making war and, if they did, whatever the outcome

285

they would surely fall prey to some Bonaparte who would begin as a dictator and end up as a tyrant. Well, the American people have known how to make war. They have waged it with unquestionable energy and fire and they did not fall into the hands of any general or Caesar. They waged the most difficult, the most terrible of all wars—civil war. They displayed all the qualities, all the virtues of a great military nation. And they waged it on an immense scale: more than a million volunteers took up arms on one side for the defense of the Union and republican institutions; on the other, to preserve their independence and local autonomy. Not a single one of these million men became the executioner of his brothers, or the satellite of a dictator. These mighty armies were led by improvised generals, many of whom deserve to be placed beside our most famous republican generals, not only because of their tactical and strategical genius, but also because they were authentic heroes, men of courage and moderation, endowed with keen political understanding and a high sense of duty as citizens. Grant and Lee, Burnside and Sherman, McClellan and Beauregard, Sheridan and Stonewall Jackson have inscribed their names in the great book of history.

I have deliberately named the best among the leaders of both armies, because I feel that high tribute is due to the American people as a whole. The two parties, the two sides have displayed the same courage, the same indomitable will, the same fearless daring, the same spirit of abnegation and of self-sacrifice. All our sympathy goes to the North, but that should not prevent us from admiring wholeheartedly the heroism shown by the South. Though it served the cause of injustice and error, it is heroism, nevertheless. It even appears that the Southerners showed greater military valor, greater energy and talent, greater spirit and brilliance than their foe, especially in the beginning. How can we help admire them, even though we deplore that such noble and rare qualities were dedicated to so unworthy a cause! What men, and also, and above all, what women! Daughters, wives, mothers, these American women of the South have revived in the middle of our nineteenth century the patriotism, the self-sacrifice, the abnegation of the women of Rome, of the most heroic period of the republic. Clelia, Cornelia, Portia had rivals in many of the towns and plantations of Louisiana and Virginia.

But such heroic military virtues seem of relatively small importance compared with the civic virtues shown by the American people in the course of this frightful war. Not a single freedom was suppressed, not a law was violated, not a voice was silenced; no guarantees were relinquished, no dictatorship was ever deemed urgent; therein lies the real miracle, the supreme victory. Look and learn, O you people of Europe, you who become panic-stricken at the slightest threat of domestic disturbances.

We must recognize, on the basis of all the evidence at hand, that legal order was maintained and respected everywhere. Without the slightest restriction or censorship, all the newspapers continued to appear. Foreign correspondents whose hostility to the Northern cause was well known, continued to send their articles to Europe without risk and without being hindered in any way. Outside of the war area, individual freedom knew no restraint, the right to free assembly was not looked upon with suspicion and no class, no one category of citizen was declared undesirable or outlawed.

This irresistible movement which is victorious in

America today is mostly the work of a novelist, on the one hand and, on the other, of a man who died on the gallows. The novel, *Uncle Tom's Cabin,* is one which nearly all of us have read and admired. The hanging, however, attracted much less attention than the novel, and only a handful among us were affected by the martyrdom of that old man, John Brown, who after having been odiously slandered, was put to death. Those who victimized him on December 2, 1859, thought at the time that the whole thing was ended. But what happened was precisely the contrary; it was only the beginning. What had ended, though, was the scandalous impunity of their murderous domination. . . .

Nothing remains to be said about Abraham Lincoln. In the middle of the nineteenth century he has provided us with a fresh example that is neither a copy nor a counterfeit of the calm, honest genius typified by Washington. He does honor to the whole of humanity as well as to the country whose destinies he led and which he sought to pacify with such wisdom and moderation. . . . Lincoln was both upright and kind, shrewd and straightforward, modest and courageous, and this blend of qualities was such as made of him a type so rare that no prince, no public figure of our century has equalled. This woodcutter who first became a lawyer and then was placed at the head of one of the greatest nations in the world has displayed all the virtues of an honest man as well as all the qualities of a statesman. No sovereign, hereditary or elective, ever spoke a language more eloquent or more worthy; none has displayed such calm and good humor, such singleness of purpose and magnanimity.

Comte de Montalembert, LA VICTOIRE DU NORD AUX ETATS-UNIS

THE DEATH OF LINCOLN

Stunned and horrified by the news of the assassination of the President, the entire world reacted immediately after the initial shock. Thousands upon thousands of messages poured into Washington from heads of state to humblest workers, and the expressions of grief and condolence gave proof of the sorrow and regret felt throughout Europe at the loss of a great man and a great leader. None, not even his bitterest foes, wished him death at the hands of an assassin. The following selections represent a brief cross-section of world response to the tragedy.

April 14, 1865

The news of course had not yet reached Victor Hugo when he wrote the following to his wife and sons:

I have just received from the President of the United States a large parcel of books and papers concerning the Civil War. . . .

COMPLETE WORKS OF VICTOR HUGO

From a Widow to a Widow

Osborne, April 29, 1865

Dear Madam:

Though a stranger to you, I cannot remain silent when so terrible a calamity has fallen upon you and your country and must personally express my *deep* and *heartfelt* sympathy with you under the shocking circumstances of your present dreadful misfortune.

No one can better *appreciate* than I can, who am myself *utterly brokenhearted* by the loss of my own beloved husband, who was the light of my life—my stay—*my all*—what your sufferings must be, and I earnestly pray that you may be supported by Him to whom alone the sorely stricken can look for comfort in this hour of heavy affliction.

With numerous expressions of true sympathy, I remain, dear Madam,

Your sincere friend,
Victoria

Jay Monaghan, DIPLOMAT IN CARPET SLIPPERS

"Tell Mrs. Lincoln That in This Little Box Is the Heart of France"

With these words Eugène Pelletan, liberal French parliamentarian, presented a commemorative gold medal to John Bigelow, American Minister to France, to be transmitted to Mrs. Lincoln. Accompanying the medal was the following message:

Madam:

On behalf of more than forty thousand French citizens, anxious to manifest their sympathies for the American Union, in the person of one of its most illustrious and purest representatives, we are instructed to offer you the medal which has been coined in honor of the great and good man whose name you bear.

If France had the freedom enjoyed by republican America, not thousands, but millions among us would have been counted as admirers of Lincoln, and believers in the opinions for which he devoted his life, and which his death has consecrated.

The medal—the cost of which was raised by popular subscription, maximum contribution two cents—was inscribed as follows:

Lincoln, an honest man; abolished slavery, saved the republic, and was assassinated the 14th of April, 1865.

Dedicated by the French democracy to Lincoln, twice elected President of the United States. Liberty! Equality! Fraternity!

John Bigelow, RETROSPECTIONS OF AN ACTIVE LIFE

From This Coarse Bark

Abraham Lincoln, a biography by a French traveler, Alphonse Joualt, was begun in Washington at the time of Lincoln's assassination, which the author witnessed.

I shall never forget the deep impression I felt when I saw come onto the platform the strange-looking great man to whom the American people had been so happy as to intrust their destinies. The gait was heavy, slow, irregular; the body long, lean, over six feet, with stooping shoulders, the long arms of a boatman, the large hands of a carpenter, extraordinary hands, with feet in proportion. . . . The turned-down shirt-collar uncovered the protruding muscles of a yellow neck, above which shot forth a mass of black hair, thick and bristling as a bunch of pine boughs; a face of irresistible attraction.

From this coarse bark emerged a forehead and eyes belonging to a superior nature. In this body was sheathed a soul wondrous by its greatness and moral beauty. On the brow, deep-furrowed with line, could be detected the thoughts and anxieties of the statesman; and in the large black eyes, deep and penetrating, whose dominant expression was good will and kindness mixed with melancholy, one discovered an inexhaustible charity, giving to the word its highest meaning, that is, perfect love for mankind.

J. J. Jusserand, WITH AMERICANS OF PAST AND PRESENT DAYS

Personal Recollections

August Laugel was a frequent contributor of stories on the Civil War to the *Revue des Deux Mondes*. He had traveled in the United States and been a guest of the President and Mrs. Lincoln. The following is an excerpt from an article dated May 15, 1865.

He [Lincoln] was most anxious to avoid involving his country in a conflict with the European powers and he used every honorable means to attain this end. Despite numerous provocations, he never addressed these countries in anything but the most friendly and restrained terms. Here he was simply obeying his innermost instinct. As a man of the West, European judgments and criticisms concerned him far less than they did his compatriots living on the Atlantic seaboard. In fact, the unvarying coolness with which he treated all that concerned Europe reveals in him a profound indifference and maybe even a slight contempt for the nations on the other side of the Atlantic. He had concentrated all his love, all his reverence upon the American people. The nation's choice, he did not claim to become her leader, nor did he wish to oppose her will. All he wanted was to walk at her side. He had the most absolute faith in the wisdom, the goodness, the courage, the fortitude and disinterestedness of his country.

August Laugel, "PERSONAL RECOLLECTIONS"

Letter from John Bright to Charles Sumner

For fifty years, I think, no other event has created such a sensation in this country as the great crime which has robbed you of your President. The whole people positively mourn, and it would seem as if again we were one nation with you, so universal is the grief, and the horror of the deed, of which Washington has been the scene. . . . In times of great excitement, dangerous men become more dangerous, partly vicious, and partly mad, and men of great mark become the objects of their hate and passion. The deed is done, and it is now too late to take precautions.

It is easy to kill a President, but it is not easy to destroy a nation.

George Macaulay Trevelyan, THE LIFE OF JOHN BRIGHT

A Hebrew prophet would have described Jehovah as sending an evil spirit to entice Wilkes Booth to his deed.

Francis, Cardinal Newman

From The Standard, *British Tory newspaper:*

He was not a hero while he lived, and therefore his cruel murder does not make him a martyr.

Prince Gortchakov to Baron de Stoeckl:

St. Petersburg, April 16-28, 1865

The telegraph has brought us the news of the double crime of which the President of the United States has fallen a victim and Mr. Seward barely escaped.

The blow which has struck Mr. Lincoln, at the very moment when he seemed about to harvest the fruits of his energy and perseverance, has been deeply felt in Russia.

Because of the absence of the Emperor I am not in a position to receive and transmit to you the expression of the sentiments of his Imperial Majesty. Being acquainted, nevertheless, with those which our august master entertains toward the United States of America, it is easy for me to realize in advance the impression which the news of this odious crime will cause his Imperial Majesty to experience.

I have hastened to testify to General Clay the earnest and cordial sympathy of the imperial cabinet with the federal government.

Please to express this in the warmest terms to President Johnson, adding thereto our most sincere wishes that this new and grievous trial not impede the onward march of the American people toward the re-establishment of the Union, and of that concord which is the source of its power and of its prosperity.

The Polish refugees in Switzerland to the great nation the republic of the United States:

Republican Citizens:

After a fatal struggle of twenty months for the independence and liberty of our country, after countless losses, we, exiles from our homes, under the aegis of the free Swiss nation, the only oasis of liberty in Europe, contemplate with hearts palpitating with emotion your gigantic struggle, supported by rights the most sacred to humanity. The news of your heroic and glorious exploits filled us with admiration, and your triumphs made us poor Poles forget our own misfortunes on beholding the great champions of liberty.

Republican citizens: Now, when the most despotic governments of old Europe are hastening to send you expressions of their sympathy, on the occasion of the horrible crime that has deprived you and all friends of liberty of its greatest defender, your President elect, Abraham Lincoln, we beg you to accept the feeble vote of sincere sympathy and profound sorrow from a few people—a handful of exiles.

Our whole nation cannot express its sentiments for you, because its people are scattered over the face of the earth; but you can accept our good wishes as the feeble echo of a friendly people.

Fraternal greeting and sympathy!

In the name of the Polish Mutual Aid Society of Geneva. . . .

From Bismarck to N. B. Judd, United States Envoy to Berlin:

Berlin, April 27, 1865

The royal government is profoundly moved by the intelligence, which reached here yesterday, of the assassination of President Lincoln, and the simultaneous attempt on the life of the Secretary of State, Mr. Seward.

In view of the so happily existing friendly relations between Prussia and the United States, the undersigned cannot forbear to express to their government the sincere sympathy of the royal government with the great loss that this crime has inflicted upon them. He therefore requests the envoy extraordinary and minister plenipotentiary of the United States of America, Mr. Judd, that he will convey the expression of these sentiments to his government, and he avails himself of this occasion, too, to renew to Mr. Judd the assurance of his distinguished consideration.

V. Bismarck

DIPLOMATIC CORRESPONDENCE, 1866

The Times *Recants*

London, April 29, 1865—A space of twenty-four hours has sufficed not only to fill the country with grief and indignation, but to evoke almost unprecedented expression of feeling from constituted bodies.

It was but on Wednesday that the intelligence of the murder reached us, and on Thursday the Houses of Lords and Commons, the Corporation of the City of London, and the people of our chief manufacturing towns in public meeting assembled had recorded their sentiments or expressed their views. In the House of Lords the absence of precedent for such a manifestation was actually made the subject of remark.

That much of this extraordinary feeling is due to the tragical character of the event and the horror with which the crime is regarded is doubtless true, nor need we dissemble the fact that the loss which the Americans have sustained is also thought our own loss in so far as one valuable guarantee for the amity of the two nations may have been thus removed. But, upon the whole, it is neither the possible embarrassment of international relations nor the infamous wickedness of the act itself which has determined public feeling. The preponderating sentiment is sincere and genuine sympathy—sorrow for the chief of a great people struck down by an assassin, and sympathy for that people in the trouble which at a crisis of their destinies such a catastrophe must bring. Abraham Lincoln was as little of a tyrant as any man who ever lived. He could have been a tyrant had he pleased, but he never uttered so much as an ill-natured speech. . . . In all America there was, perhaps, not one man who less deserved to be the victim of this revolution than he who has just fallen.

E. D. *Adams,* GREAT BRITAIN AND THE AMERICAN CIVIL WAR

The Italian Society of United Mechanics of
Turin, to citizen George Perkins Marsh,
United States Envoy to Italy:

The Italian Society of United Mechanics of Turin, which is proud to have Giuseppe Garibaldi as honorary president, the man who contended in Italy for the triumph of that same principle for which Abraham Lincoln was assassinated, cannot remain silent on this great occasion.

Impressed with profound sorrow for the misfortunes of the United States of America, the officers of our society beg you to act as our interpreter to your countrymen, to express to them our high regard, particularly for one mechanic like us, who was born in Kentucky, and whose genius elevated him to the highest rank in the nation that trusted its destiny to his care; who served his country so well that the enemies of all good were forced to arm the hand of a hired assassin to take his precious life.

May free America find a successor worthy of Abraham Lincoln, and may the Monroe doctrine prevail for the good of the country.

Given in Turin, in the Society hall, the 30th of April, 1865.

DIPLOMATIC CORRESPONDENCE, 1866

Marx-Engels Correspondence Concluded

Marx to Engels:

May 1, 1865

The *chivalry of the South* ends worthily. In this connection the assassination of Lincoln was the greatest
piece of folly that they could commit. *Johnson* is
stern, inflexible, revengeful and as a former poor
white has a deadly hatred of the oligarchy. He will
stand less on ceremony with the fellows, and through
the assassination he finds the temper of the North
adequate to his intentions.

Marx and Engels, THE CIVIL WAR IN THE UNITED STATES

Oscar de Lafayette to the United States Minister in Paris:

Chavaniac, May 2, 1865

Sir: I hope you will excuse me for addressing you this
little note; but you will certainly think it natural
that a member of the Lafayette family should wish to
join the citizens of the United States in their mourning. At the time the odious crime was committed I
was absent from Paris, and was sick; so it was impossible to unite with some of my countrymen in their
public expressions of sorrow for the death of the
eminent American statesman.

I now express all my regrets, and ask you to accept
my personal esteem.

Your obedient servant,

Oscar de Lafayette

Resolution from the Covent Garden Theatrical Fund to Charles Francis Adams:

May 4, 1865

Resolved, That this honorable corporation, the
Covent Garden Theatrical Fund, desires to give utterance to the feelings of grief and horror with which
it has received the fearful intelligence of the assassination of Abraham Lincoln, President of the United
States, and to convey to his sorrowing widow and the
American people its profound condolence and sympathy, together with the expression of its sad and
solemn regret that the unnatural parricide who deprived the Father of his country of existence, and the
wife of his bosom of her loved protector, should in
any the slightest way have been connected with the
profession this corporation represents, whose honor
and loyalty have ever been its most cherished pride.

The University of Perugia to the representative of the United States near the Italian government:

We, the committee of the students of the University of Perugia, respectfully request you to convey
to your government the feelings excited in our breasts

by the intelligence of the assassination of Mr. Lincoln, and the attack on Mr. Seward.

These two great men, who, with General Grant, completed the great work of emancipation begun by Young America, deserve our greatest admiration and our most sincere thanks.

As our opinions are not influenced by fear or political expediency, and as sincerity is common to young minds, we hope it will not be thought improper that we should join our voices to those of all Europe in detestation of the horrid crime that robbed the republic of the United States of its illustrious chief, whose death we mourn with all lovers of liberty.

We hope that the spirit of enterprise will revive with renewed vigor after the term of sorrow, and that the martyr's blood may prove a pledge for future victories.

We have our martyrs too! Let not America forget that she has our sympathy, and let her people remember that we weep with them in their misfortunes.

Attested by the rector of the University, this 11th day of May, 1865.

DIPLOMATIC CORRESPONDENCE, 1866

The Death of Lincoln

You lay a wreath on murdered Lincoln's bier
You, who with mocking pencil wont to trace
Broad for the self-complacent British sneer
His length of shambling limb, his furrowed face.

302

Yes, he had lived to shame me from my sneer
To lame my pencil and confute my pen—
To make me own this hind of princes peer,
This rail-splitter, a true-born king of men.

Tom Taylor, PUNCH

Letter from Prosper Mérimée to Sir Anthony Panizzi:

May 12, 1865

What with all the *fuss* that's being made over Mr. Lincoln's death and all the messages of sympathy we are sending them, and with the Queen of England and the Empress writing to the widow with their own lily-white hands, the arrogance of those rascals who already think of themselves as the biggest frogs in the pond is going to become quite unbearable. Be prepared for the most impudent swagger on their part. Lincoln was certainly a poor enough wretch. But he had some sound good sense in his head and he had learned quite a lot in the course of the last four years.

Maurice Parturier, ed., COLLECTED LETTERS OF PROSPER MÉRIMÉE

The Assassination of Abraham Lincoln

The manuscript of this poem by Henrik Ibsen was dated Rome, April 30, 1865, and first appeared in the Danish newspaper *The Fatherland* on May 15, 1865.

A gun was fired in western land,
And Europe was shaken and shocked.
There were fear and confusion on every hand
Within the ribanded flock.
O Europe, you ancient, with order and guide,
With law for each step and sail,
With shining escutcheon and helmet bright,
With virtuous judgment for sin and night,
You turned so remarkably pale.

On letters are eagles and unicorn
In mourning's wax and seal.
The mailboat sounds its shrill, sharp horn;
Dispatches on road and on keel.
The cotton magnate, Old Glory's son,
And mobs in the land of the lie,
Were straining to reach their peace-hope's palm,
When came this shot in the silence and calm,
And a lonely man had to die.

And then they were frightened, Old Europe's breed;
But what were they frightened by?
A Prussian action a Dybböl deed
They saw, yet they heaved not a sigh.
A raven will not its kindred hack;
Yet Poland you will recall?—
The English navy as bandit pack,
The grave at Flensburg, the Union Jack—
Why now does this deed you appall?

Yon fiery rose that blossoms red
And frightens you with its blood,—
On Europe's stem it has grown and fed,
Though the western soil was good.
You planted the sapling, which now is lush

And flames on America's crest.
Yes, Europe has tied, with its own long hand,
That martyrdom's crimson-hued knighthood band
On Abraham Lincoln's breast! . . .

Translated by Dr. Theodore Jorgenson

A Message from Descendants of Slaves

Concord Lodge, London
May 22, 1865

To the Citizen Andrew Johnson
President of the Republic of the United States, thrice
greeting:

Stricken by the ball of a serf of tyranny, Abraham
Lincoln is dead—victim to his love for the cause of
our brethren, the black laborers of the southern
States.

Descendants of slaves, it is with feverish anxiety
that we have followed the great movements of the
drama of emancipation, for which the blood of the
upholders of right has been shed. Independent operatives, our bosoms have swelled with joy at the news
of the downfall of oppression beneath the heroic
efforts of the soldiers of emancipation.

Our brethren are free! Slavery is abolished! Such
is the cry which, throughout the Old World, the
downtrodden of our day repeated with joy, when the
death of the great martyr came to add new brilliancy
to the glorious halo which surrounds the sacred cause
of right and of justice.

Mourning is in our hearts! Our grief is great! We

weep with you for the loss of the great citizen who represented the nation of freemen. Faithful to his memory, we shall tell our sons of the actions of this just man, who has passed from this life to the life immortal.

> *L. Lubay, President of Concord Lodge; P. Bordage, Secretary; Lardon, Orator; L. Pairier, 1st Supervisor; L. Ridet, 2nd Supervisor; Le Roux, Treasurer; Emile Hattorff, Expert; Azerna, Architect.*

DIPLOMATIC CORRESPONDENCE, 1866

The End of Slavery

Brief passages from a notebook kept by Victor Hugo during a Rhine journey, September-October, 1865:

Two dead men have killed slavery. What John Brown's death had initiated, Lincoln's death brought to completion.

These two murderers, Wyse's in 1859, Booth's in 1865, unintentionally played the role of liberators, the one by setting up the gallows and the other by drawing his dagger. The guiding principle of their act, slavery erect, and, so to speak pilloried between two murders, was thus revealed.

On April 29, 1865, Hugo sent a letter in care of the American Minister to

Belgium addressed to "My Fellow Citizens, the World." In this letter he expressed his sorrow at the assassination of Lincoln.

The thunderclap at Washington has shaken the earth. . . . How frightful a cataclysm! . . . The American people is a colossus of bronze; traitors may scratch its surface, but they cannot overthrow it. . . . America has become the guide among the nations . . . the nation pointing out to its sister nations the granite way to liberty and to universal brotherhood.

A Devoted Citizen of the Republic of Mankind

COMPLETE WORKS OF VICTOR HUGO

BIBLIOGRAPHY
AND ACKNOWLEDGMENTS

"I Fall on My Knees, Weeping." Victor Hugo, "Appeal for John Brown," in *Letters on American Slavery*. Boston: Anti-Slavery Society, 1860. All other Hugo selections from *Complete Works of Victor Hugo*. Paris: L'Edition de l'Imprimerie Nationale. II. Paul Ollendorff and Albin Michel. (Translated by Tina du Bouchet.)

There Is No Such Thing As Distance Today. Count Agénor de Gasparin, *America Before Europe*. New York: Charles Scribner, 1862.

The Signal Has Been Given; and letters throughout. Karl Marx and Frederick Engels, *The Civil War in the United States*. New York: International Publishers, 1937.

Domestic Gossip to People Enjoying a Revolution. Gordon N. Ray, ed., *Letters and Private Papers of William Makepeace Thackeray*. Cambridge: Harvard University Press, 1946. (Reprinted by permission of Mrs. Dickenson, Receiver of the Estate of Mrs. Helena Makepeace Thackeray Fuller.)

"I Do Not See How the United States Can Be Cobbled Together Again." Letters from Lord Russell to Lord Lyons, in E.D. Adams, *Great Britain and the American Civil War*. New York: Longmans, Green & Co., 1925.

A Russian Observation. Letter from Baron de Brunow to Prince Gortchakov, in E.D. Adams, *Great Britain and the American Civil War*. New York: Longmans, Green & Co., 1925.

A British View of American Aristocracy. Marquess of Lothian, *The Confederate Secession*. Edinburgh and London: William Blackwood & Sons, 1864.

Slavery Corrupts the Soul. Elysèe Reclus, *Revue des Deux Mondes*. Paris: December, 1860; January, 1861.

The United States Can Never Exist Again. Alexander J. Beresford-Hope, *A Popular View of the American Civil War*. London: 1861.

Verse. *Punch*. London: March 30, 1861. (By permission of *Punch*.)

"I Had Many Reasons For Declining the Mission." William Howard Russell, in John Bigelow, *Retrospections of an Active Life*. New York: Baker & Taylor, 1909.

A Russian Diplomat Reports. Baron de Stoeckl to Prince Gortchakov; and letters throughout. Albert Woldman, *Lincoln and the Russians*. Cleveland: World Publishing Company, 1952.

Two Presidents and a Disastrous Rout. William Howard Russell, *The Civil War in America*. Boston: Gardner A. Fuller, 1861; E.D. Adams, *Great Britain and the American Civil War*. New York: Longmans, Green & Co., 1925; and John Bigelow, *Retrospections of an Active Life*. New York: Baker & Taylor, 1909.

Side Lights on Bull Run. *The History of the London Times.* New York: The Macmillan Company, 1939.

These Armies Differed from Ours. Comte de Paris, *History of the Civil War in America.* Philadelphia: Porter & Coates, 1875.

The Republic of San Marino Confers Citizenship on President Lincoln. Letter from the Regent Captain of the Republic of San Marino, 1861.

Hatred Prevailed. Maurice Sand, *Six Mille Lieues à Toute Vapeur.* Paris: Michel-Lévy frères, 1862. (Translated by Tina du Bouchet.)

"It Is Out of My Line." Francis Darwin, *Life and Letters of Charles Darwin.* New York: D. Appleton & Co., 1887.

"Surely These People Are Not Slaves?" Samuel Phillips Day, *Down South.* London: Hurst & Blackett, 1862.

Prussia Is Disturbed by the Conflict. Letter from Baron de Schlenitz to Baron von Grabow. *Diplomatic Correspondence,* 1862.

A Little-Known Moment in History. H. Nelson Gay, "Lincoln's Offer of a Command to Garibaldi," *Century Magazine,* (November, 1907–April, 1908). Also Howard R. Marraro, "Lincoln's Offer of a Command to Garibaldi." Springfield: *Illinois State Historical Journal,* (September, 1943). (By permission of Illinois State Historical Society.)

Two Countries, Placed at the Extremities of Two Worlds. Letter from Prince Gortchakov to Baron de Stoeckl. *Diplomatic Correspondence*, 1862.

The Level of Human Values Has Fallen. Prince Napoleon, *Voyage aux États-Unis et au Canada*. Paris: *Revue de Paris*, September, 1933.

"I Feel for My Friends Both North and South." Letter from Fredrika Bremer, in Signe A. Rooth, *Seeress of the Northland*. Philadelphia: American Swedish Historical Foundation, 1955. (By permission of Signe A. Rooth.)

A Creation of Human Reason. Eugène Forcade, "Chronique de la Quinzaine" in *Revue des Deux Mondes*. Paris: August 15 and September 15, 1861. (Translated by Tina du Bouchet.)

General Frémont Acts as Proconsul. Camille Ferri Pisani, *Prince Napoleon in America, 1861*, translated by George J. Joyaux. Bloomington, Indiana: Indiana University Press, 1959. (By permission of Indiana University Press.)

Contrasting Points of View. William Howard Russell, *My Diary North and South*. London: Bradbury & Evans, 1863. Also August Laugel, *Les États-Unis Pendant la Guerre*. Paris: 1866.

"I Would Walk Barefoot to the End of the Earth." J.A. Hobson, *Richard Cobden, The International Man*. London: Ernest Benn, Ltd., 1918. Also John Bigelow, *Retrospections of an Active Life*. New York: Baker & Taylor, 1909.

Happy Results to the Safety of Europe. Sir Edward Bulwer-Lytton, in John Bigelow, *Retrospections of an Active Life*. New York: Baker & Taylor, 1909.

Men and Angels Must Weep. Anthony Trollope, *North America*. New York: Alfred A. Knopf, Inc., 1951.

Letters from King Leopold to Queen Victoria. A.C. Benson and Viscount Esher, eds., *Letters of Queen Victoria*. London: John Murray, 1907; and George Earle Buckle, ed., *Letters of Queen Victoria*. London: John Murray, 1926. Second Series.

"We Have No Troubles But Public Troubles." J.W. Cross, ed., *George Eliot's Life As Related in Her Letters*. Edinburgh: William Blackwood & Sons.

The Trent Affair. John Bright, *A Friendly Voice from England on American Affairs*. New York: William C. Bryant & Co., 1862; letters from John Bright to Charles Sumner, *Proceedings of the Massachusetts Historical Society* (Boston), XLV, 1912. (By permission of Massachusetts Historical Society.)

"I Shall Find This Hating You Very Hard Work." Francis Darwin, *Life and Letters of Charles Darwin*. New York: D. Appleton & Co., 1887.

"I Can Make No War in My Soul." Letters from Robert Browning, in Henry James, *William Wetmore Story and His Friends*. Edinburgh: William Blackwood & Sons, 1903.

If All Other Tongues Are Silent. John Bright, *A Friendly Voice from England on American Affairs*. New York: William C. Bryant & Co., 1862.

A Turning Point, for Good or Evil. *Autobiography of John Stuart Mill*. New York: Columbia University Press, 1924. (By permission of Columbia University Press.)

Palmerston Sends an Early New Year Greeting to the Queen. John Bigelow, *Retrospections of an Active Life*. New York: Baker & Taylor, 1909.

Enlistments and Emigration. Ella Lonn, *Foreigners in the Union Army and Navy*. Baton Rouge, Louisiana: Louisiana State University Press, 1951. (By permission of the Louisiana State University Press); and *Diplomatic Correspondence, 1864–1865*.

"Our Government Is Made Up of Men Drawn from the Aristocratic Families." Letter from John Bright, in John Bigelow, *Retrospections of an Active Life*. New York: Baker & Taylor, 1909.

As Though God Had Forsaken Them. George Sand, *Correspondance Complète*. Paris: Calmann-Lévy, 1883; also Preface to *Uncle Tom's Cabin*. Paris: Michel-Lévy frères, 1862.

A View From Pennsylvania Avenue. Edward Dicey, *Six Months in the Federal States*. London: Macmillan & Co., Ltd., 1863.

"I Am in a Minority." Letters from Richard Monckton Milnes, in *Massachusetts Historical Society Pro-*

314

ceedings (Boston), XLV, 1912. (By permission of Massachusetts Historical Society); and in T. Wemyss Reid, *The Life, Letters and Friendships of Richard Monckton Milnes.* New York: Cassell Publishing Company, 1891.

"You Poor Mad Things—What Will Become of You?" *Letters of John Ruskin,* eds., E.T. Cook and Alexander Wedderburn. London: George Allen, 1909.

"To My American Friends . . ." Letter from Fredrika Bremer, in Signe A. Rooth, *Seeress of the Northland.* Philadelphia: American Swedish Foundation, 1955. (By permission of Signe A. Rooth.)

The Catholic Church Deplores Slavery. Letter from Monsignor Dupanloup to his clergy, in Comte de Montalembert, *La Victorie du Nord aux États-Unis.* Paris: E. Dentu, 1866. (Translated by Tina du Bouchet.)

Death Under a Rose Bush. Prince de Joinville, *Guerre d'Amerique—Campagne de Potomac.* Paris: Michel-Lévy frères, 1863. (Translated by Tina du Bouchet.)

Britain Comes to the Defense of Southern Womanhood. Letter from Lord Palmerston to Charles F. Adams, in *Massachusetts Historical Society Proceedings* (Boston), XLV, 1912. (By permission of Massachusetts Historical Society); also letter from Lord Russell to Lord Palmerston, in E.D. Adams, *Great*

Britain and the American Civil War. New York: Longmans, Green & Co., 1925.

The Ball Opens. Heros von Borcke, *Memoirs of the Confederate War for Independence.* London: 1866.

The Continent Divided Is Inconceivable. Letter from Comte de Paris to M. Buloz. (Published by courtesy of Alfred Krebs and translated by Tina du Bouchet.)

Texas for Barter. Letter from M. Theron to Governor F.R. Lubbock, *Diplomatic Correspondence,* 1863–1864; also letter from Drouyn de Lhuys to William Dayton, *Diplomatic Correspondence,* 1864–1865.

The Effects of Intervention. Edouard Laboulaye, "The United States and France," *Boston Daily Advertiser,* October, 1862.

Europe Has Been Most Profoundly Deceived. Letter from Alfred de Vigny, in Henri Guillemin, "Vigny and the Yankees." Paris: *Le Monde,* March 5, 1955. (By permission of M. Henri Guillemin and translated by Tina du Bouchet.)

Intermission at a Ball. Heros von Borcke, *Memoirs of the Confederate War for Independence,* London: 1866.

Look at Their Wild Ways . . . Donaldson Jordan and Edwin J. Pratt, *Europe and the American Civil War.* Boston: Houghton Mifflin Company, 1931.

Palmerston and Russell Consider Mediation. Spencer Walpole, *The Life of Lord John Russell.* London:

Longmans, Green & Co., 1889; and E.D. Adams, *Great Britain and the American Civil War*. New York: Longmans, Green & Co., 1925.

"Your Revolution Is Ridiculous and Not Tragic Enough," and subsequent letters. Maurice Parturier, ed., *Collected Letters of Prosper Mérimée*. Toulouse: Edouard Privat, 1957, 1958. (Translated by Tina du Bouchet.)

The Cotton Burners of America and the Lancashire Sufferers. Peter Sinclair, *Freedom or Slavery in the United States*. London: 1862.

Proposals Will Be Made to Russia. E.A. Adamov, "Russia and the United States at the Time of the Civil War," *Journal of Modern History*, December, 1930. Chicago: University of Chicago Press. (By permission of University of Chicago Press.)

"The South Has Not My Sympathies." John Morley, *The Life of William Ewart Gladstone*. New York: The Macmillan Company, 1903. (By permission of the Executrix of Mr. Guy Morley.)

A Vile Speech at Newcastle. Letter from John Bright to Charles Sumner, *Proceedings of the Massachusetts Historical Society* (Boston), XLVI, 1913. (By permission of Massachusetts Historical Society.)

An Evaluation of Lincoln. Karl Marx, "On the Civil War and Lincoln," *Political Affairs*. New York: February, 1959. (By permission of *Political Affairs* and translated by Amy Schechter.)

Two Races Enclosed In a Single Arena. [Attributed to Feodor Dostoevsky.] Vremya: 1861. (Translated by Amy Schechter.)

Letter from the Workingmen of Manchester to President Lincoln. *Manchester Guardian,* January 1, 1863.

"I Would Have a 'Te Deum' Not a 'Miserere' Sung." Letter from Fredrika Bremer, in Signe A. Rooth, *Seeress of the Northland.* Philadelphia: American Swedish Historical Association, 1955. (By permission of Signe A. Rooth.)

Editorial from the St. Petersburg *Vedomosti,* January, 1863. *Diplomatic Correspondence,* 1864.

Italian Liberals Hail the Emancipation Proclamation. Albert Woldman, *Lincoln and the Russians.* Cleveland: World Publishing Company, 1952.

Emancipation Is But a Pretext. Alphonse de Lamartine, *Cours Familier de Littérature.* Paris: 1856–1865, XX. (Translated by Tina du Bouchet.)

Napoleon III Speaks Frankly. *Appleton's Annual Encyclopedia, 1863.* New York: D. Appleton & Co., 1864; and John Bigelow, *Retrospections of an Active Life.* New York: Baker & Taylor, 1909.

France Suffers from the Blockade. *Revue des Deux Mondes;* and Jules and Edmond de Goncourt, *Mémoires de la Vie Littéraire.*

French Cotton Workers Oppose Intervention. Eugène Forcade, "Chronique de la Quinzaine" in *Revue des Deux Mondes*. Paris: February 1, 1863. (Translated by Tina du Bouchet.)

"Our Country Accepts with Gratitude." Resolution of thanks, in "Report of the American International Relief Committee for the Suffering Operatives of Great Britain." New York: C.A. Alvord, 1864.

Song of the Unemployed Cotton Workers. E.D. Adams, *Great Britain and the American Civil War*. New York: Longmans, Green & Co., 1925.

Letter from John Ruskin to Charles Eliot Norton. *Letters of John Ruskin*, eds., E.T. Cook and Alexander Wedderburn. London: George Allen, 1909.

Appeal from the Protestant Pastors of France. *Diplomatic Correspondence*, 1864.

The Emancipation Proclamation Strengthens Anti-Slavery Feeling in England. Edward L. Pierce, "Letters of Richard Cobden to Charles Sumner," *American Historical Review*, II, (1896–1897). (By permission of American Historical Association.)

Letter from Charles Darwin to Asa Gray. Francis Darwin, *Life and Letters of Charles Darwin*. New York: D. Appleton & Co., 1887.

Letter from John Bright to John Greenleaf Whittier. Samuel T. Pickard, *Life and Letters of John Greenleaf Whittier*. Boston: Houghton Mifflin Company, 1894.

The Finger of Providence. Canon de Haerne, *The American Question*. London: 1863.

319

Privilege Curses the American Republic. George Macaulay Trevelyan, *Life of John Bright*. Boston: Houghton Mifflin Company, 1913. (By permission of G. M. Trevelyan.)

Disraeli Looks into the Future. W.F. Monypenny and George E. Buckle, *Life of Benjamin Disraeli, Earl of Beaconsfield*. London: John Murray, 1910.

Southern Aid Movement in England. *Diplomatic Correspondence*, 1864–1865.

Death of General Stuart. Heros von Borcke, *Memoirs of the Confederate War for Independence*. London: 1866.

"Can We Make These Men Our Friends?" George Macaulay Trevelyan, *Life of John Bright*. Boston: Houghton Mifflin Company, 1913. (By permission of G.M. Trevelyan.)

The Gaieties That Were Going On. FitzGerald Ross, *Cities and Camps of the Confederate States*, ed., R.B. Harwell. Bloomington: Indiana University Press, 1958. (By permission of Indiana University Press.)

"I Have No Dislike of the Negroes." Letters from Thomas Carlyle, in Moncure D. Conway, *Autobiography*. Boston: Houghton Mifflin Company, 1904.

For Peace in America. A petition from the people of Great Britain and Ireland. *Diplomatic Correspondence*, 1864.

"My Heart Goes with the South, and My Head with the North." Leonard Huxley, *Life and Letters of*

Thomas Henry Huxley. New York: D. Appleton and Co., 1901.

Twelve French Patriots of Tours. Beckles Willson, *John Slidell and the Confederates in Paris*. New York: Minton-Balch, 1932.

Hypocrisy in the North. Duvergier de Hauranne, "Letters and Travel Notes," in *Revue des Deux Mondes*. Paris: August 15, 1865. (Translated by Tina du Bouchet.)

Persevere, Illustrious President! *Diplomatic Correspondence*, 1865.

A Reminder from the British Foreign Office. A communiqué from Lord Russell to the Confederate agents in Europe. *Diplomatic Correspondence*, 1866.

A Noble Page in the History of Great Men. Letter from Monsignor Dupanloup to Augustin Cochin, in Comte de Montalembert, *La Victoire du Nord aux États-Unis*. Paris: E. Dentu, 1866. (Translated by Tina du Bouchet.)

Letter from William Howard Russell, in John Bigelow, *Retrospections of an Active Life*. New York: Baker & Taylor, 1909.

Spaniards Take Hope. Citizens of Spain hail the Northern victories. *Diplomatic Correspondence*, 1865.

When Darkness Fell. Marquis Adolphe de Chambrun, *Impressions of Lincoln and the Civil War*. New York: Random House, Inc., 1952.

Memo to the Queen. *Memoirs of Prince Choldwig von Hohenlohe-Schillingsfurst.* London: William Heinemann, Ltd., 1906.

A Blank Page for What Concerns America. John Bigelow, *Retrospections of an Active Life.* New York: Baker & Taylor, 1909.

Sir Edward Bulwer-Lytton on Lee's Surrender. John Bigelow, *Retrospections of an Active Life.* New York: Baker & Taylor, 1909.

Mazzini on the Northern Victory. Donaldson Jordan and Edwin J. Pratt, *Europe and the American Civil War.* Boston: Houghton Mifflin Company, 1931.

Young America's Teachings Will Not Be Lost on Old Europe. Address from the people of Brussels to Ambassador Sanford. *Diplomatic Correspondence,* 1866.

"Look and Learn, O You People of Europe." Comte de Montalembert, *La Victoire du Nord aux États-Unis.* Paris: E. Dentu, 1866. (Translated by Tina du Bouchet.)

The Death of Lincoln. From a Widow to a Widow. Jay Monaghan, *Diplomat in Carpet Slippers.* Indianapolis: Bobbs-Merrill Co., Inc., 1945; "Tell Mrs. Lincoln That in This Little Box Is the Heart of France." John Bigelow, *Retrospections of an Active Life.* New York: Baker & Taylor, 1909; From This Coarse Bark. Alphonse Joualt, in J.J. Jusserand, *With Americans of Past and Present Days.* New York: August Laugel, in *Revue des Deux Mondes,* May 15, Charles Scribner's Sons, 1917; Personal Recollections,

1865, (translated by Tina du Bouchet); Letter from John Bright to Charles Sumner. George Macaulay Trevelyan, *The Life of John Bright*. Boston: Houghton Mifflin Company, 1913. (By permission of G.M. Trevelyan); The *Times* Recants. E.D. Adams, *Great Britain and the American Civil War*. New York: Longmans, Green & Co., 1925; "The Death of Lincoln." Poem by Tom Taylor, in *Punch*. London: May 6, 1865. (By permission of *Punch*); The Assassination of Abraham Lincoln. Poem by Henrik Ibsen, in *The Fatherland*, May 15, 1865. (By permission of and translated by Dr. Theodore Jorgenson); Remarks and Letters of Condolence; *Diplomatic Correspondence*, 1866.

EUROPE LOOKS AT THE CIVIL WAR

This book was first published in October, 1960. It was composed, printed and bound by The Haddon Craftsmen, Inc., of Scranton, Pennsylvania, and designed by Wladislaw Finne.

BELLE BECKER SIDEMAN
AND LILLIAN FRIEDMAN

Belle Becker Sideman was for several years managing
editor of Random House. She was the co-editor of *Bedside Book of Famous French Stories*. Lillian Friedman,
a vice president of Brentano's, has been a bookseller for
over twenty years. She has written a book column for
St. Louis and San Francisco newspapers.

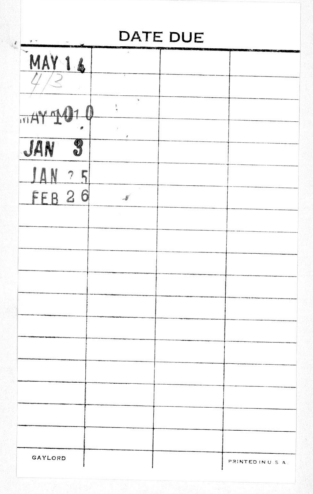